# Life After Eden

## When SIN Left Us Naked

# Heather Thompson Day
# Seth Michael Day

**Pacific Press®**
Publishing Association

Nampa, Idaho | Oshawa, Ontario, Canada
www.pacificpress.com

Cover design by Steve Lanto
Cover design resources from iStockphoto.com
Inside design by Aaron Troia

The authors assume full responsibility for the accuracy of all facts and quotations as cited in this book.

You can obtain additional copies of this book by calling toll-free 1-800-765-6955 or by visiting http://www.adventistbookcenter.com.

Library of Congress Cataloging-in-Publication Data

Names: Day, Heather Thompson, author.
Title: Life after Eden : when sin left us naked / Heather Thompson Day and
   Seth Michael Day.
Description: Nampa : Pacific Press Publishing, 2016.
Identifiers: LCCN 2016026040 | ISBN 9780816361700 (pbk.)
Subjects: LCSH: Christian life—Meditations.
Classification: LCC BV4501.3 .D395 2016 | DDC 242/.2—dc23 LC record available at
https://lccn.loc.gov/2016026040

August 2016

# Dedication

This book is dedicated to London, Hudson, and Sawyer. Thank you for allowing us to understand a small fraction of how much God loves us. Nothing has molded, shaped, or stretched our character quite like parenthood. If God never gives us another answered prayer, you three will have been enough.

Love,

Mom and Dad

# Contents

Introduction ............................................................. 7

**Day 1**   In the Beginning . . . ...................................... 9

**Day 2**   Adam: From Glory to Fig................................... 17

**Day 3**   Eve of the Fall ................................................ 24

**Day 4**   From Adam to Ashes........................................ 32

**Day 5**   When God Says No .......................................... 39

**Day 6**   Caskets and Thorns.......................................... 51

**Day 7**   Making Room.................................................. 57

**Day 8**   Divide and Conquer ........................................ 62

**Day 9**   What Is Truth? ................................................ 68

**Day 10**   The View From Rock Bottom ............................ 73

**Day 11**   I Won't Be Staying Long .................................. 77

**Day 12**   Life Is but a Moment ...................................... 83

**Day 13**   Set Your Alarm................................................ 88

**Day 14**   And It Begins Again . . . .................................. 96

**Day 15**   The Church Reformers...................................... 102

**Day 16**   A Hill Worth Dying On .................................. 109

**Day 17**   But It Was Empty ............................................ 114

**Day 18**   Comatose........................................................ 119

**Day 19**   Dear Adulterer ................................................ 123

**Day 20**     A Sinner's Touch ............................................... 128

**Day 21**     God Is Not Coming Back to Save a Church.................... 133

**Day 22**     If I Were the Devil ............................................ 140

**Day 23**     Heaven: Why Can't Everyone Go? ..................... 144

**Day 24**     Is God Enough? Part 1 .................................... 150

**Day 25**     The Night I Called Off My Wedding ............... 155

**Day 26**     Is God Enough? Part 2: Being a Martyr.......... 164

**Day 27**     Secret Admirer ............................................... 170

**Day 28**     Life After Naked ........................................... 177

**Day 29**     Dear Cancer: You Are Dying............................ 183

**Day 30**     Epilogue: Stepping Back in Eden ..................... 190

# Introduction

Parking your car, you take one more look in the rearview mirror before exiting your vehicle. When your feet hit the pavement, a deep swallow of breath stings going down. *It's a cold night,* you think to yourself while walking to the door a bit faster than usual. Once inside, you stroll across the room. The nerves are firing, so you take a deep breath. There are a lot of people here, and the music is blaring. You use your arms when you talk and tell jokes that leave the room in a roar. All eyes are on you, and it feels good to be noticed. It feels right to be seen. You were made for this.

Then, you overhear whispers. They can't believe how brazen you are. They are shocked at the ease of your exposure. Fumbling backward a bit, you take another gulp of air that's too cold for your lungs; it burns, and you no longer want to be noticed. Suddenly you are blushing and you can't understand why. You try desperately to use your hands to cover yourself, but it's no use. You are naked, and this isn't a party.

Oftentimes we convince ourselves that sin is a sneaky villain that is hard to detect and crawls in and out of our lives unseen. We are fooling ourselves. We have never been more raw and visible, and it doesn't take a magnifying glass to recognize how exposed to the elements we really are. Our flesh is bare, our skin is undecorated, and try as we may to convince ourselves that life is a party, it's of no use. Every mirror reveals the cold, hard truth. Every reflection conveys the death lurking beneath our shadows.

We buy suits and dresses, scarves and ties, hats and coats to cover up the shame we have been feeling since Eden. This world is no rose-colored garden. How dare we ever grow numb to this cold? This is "life after naked."

7

## Day 1 — Heather

# In the Beginning . . .

Absolute nakedness was intrusive, confusing to the senses.
Paradoxically, it both revealed and diminished identity.
—P. D. James

Sometimes I wonder what Eden must have been like.

When I was a kid, I started writing a book from Adam's perspective. It opened with Adam taking his first breath of cold and yet soothing air. It filled his lungs, never burned them. It depicted a perfect man walking in a perfect Eden, feeling overwhelmed by the sounds, the smells, the beauty. What do you think the sky looked like in Eden? I wonder if it was blue, or a myriad different colors all bursting from the seams at the same time. Maybe that is why God made His promise with Noah that He would never flood the earth again by flashing a rainbow. Perhaps it was a reminder of Eden, and a promise that one day they'd be able to see the colors they'd been told about. It's possible, isn't it? I bet birds and crickets literally sang like the New York Mass Choir. I bet when Adam first saw Eve, he cried.

I wonder what Eve looked like—the perfect woman. Maybe she was a blond. Perhaps that is why my entire childhood was filled with daydreaming about dying my brown hair blond, showing up at school the next day, and making all the boys fall backward in their chairs. Or maybe Eve was a brunette. Maybe she had the long, perfect, thick, wavy dark hair that only beautiful foreign models put brushes in. I bet her breasts were perfect. I bet her thighs were toned with slight hints of athletic muscle that she

9

never had to work for. I bet her teeth were white, but not the type of white that we know, a glorious, holy white. I wonder if her smile was mischievous, if one grin toward Adam made him beg her for more. I wonder if he ever held her close to his side while watching stars at night. If they talked about plans and dreams while watching stars dance across the sky. I have a feeling that in Eden, they never made a wish, because everything they could ever want was shimmering right before them.

And then, they sinned and they discovered their nakedness. I can assure you that there were nights that Adam woke up screaming. I can see him ripping open his once-protected eyes and crying. I bet the first time he gulped air on a bitterly cold day and felt it burn his lungs, he sobbed. I can just see him beating his chest when leaves fell from trees and flowers withered. I bet faded leaves looked a lot like the jaded world he was living in. I bet Adam wanted to die long before his head fell to the grave. I wonder if Adam was the first person to ever contemplate suicide? Here, this perfect man is the father of the world's first murderer, Cain. I wonder if Adam could even fathom murder, if he just kept shaking his head, trying to make the logic add up but it never did. I wonder if Adam and Eve blamed themselves for what happened to Abel.

After the Fall, after swallowing that large lump of sin that never did quite seem to go down, I bet Adam and Eve fought. I bet they went to bed many nights not speaking. I bet she whimpered softly into her pillow, and he pretended not to hear her. I bet he tried touching her side in the middle of the night and she rolled closer to the wall. I bet there were moments when Adam and Eve couldn't look at each other without feeling anger. I wonder if they had flashbacks to nights in Eden, laughing, and staring at dancing stars; and when they came back to reality, tiny pieces of their hearts died, slowly. I bet they missed the small things the most. The birds that sounded like flutes, the banjo of the crickets, the warmth of a perfect wind. I bet they missed the color white. I bet they'd be horrified to see how much we cling to life after naked.

"In the beginning God created the heavens and the earth. Now the earth was formless and empty, darkness was over the surface of the deep, and the Spirit of God was hovering over the waters. And God said, 'Let there be light,' and there was light" (Genesis 1:1–3). I often have to remind myself of the first few lines in Genesis—it is where I draw my strength.

As I sat down at the computer in my office, I shifted to face the beautiful window that stares out onto the college campus where I am a faculty member. The sign on my door confirms that. My job is to take unbridled young minds and try my hardest to transform them. My favorite quote on education essentially says that it is our (the instructors') purpose to turn mirrors into windows. Mirrors reflect our own thoughts, perspectives, and ideologies. Windows open us to the rest of the world. My job is to take a generation of social-media zombies and get them to stop thinking about their next 140-character tweet long enough to realize that there is a whole world out there—and they are not the center of it.

This adult generation is searching for something. We are the most medicated, intoxicated, overweight adult cohort in US history. The epidemic that ails the population today, which claims to be connected, is a dire feeling of loneliness. We have rewired our brains to think that we have to share in order to be human. Long gone are the days of deep personal thought and self-examination. Now we share publicly in order to feel alive. We must always be connected, and yet many of us feel alone. In every head focused on a cell phone screen during dinner, I see a walking mirror. A generation with headphones on hand at all times, because—how could we ever take the time to actually listen to someone? And so we are connected, and yet we are lonely.

So today, I faced my window. I wanted to write something hopeful for you, and so I shifted my position. I can see the campus ablaze with students walking to and from their classes. Hundreds of different perspectives and life stories are an arm's reach away. Windows change the way I write and the way I think. If only we lived in a world filled with windows.

When I got to my computer, however, I saw I had seventeen new emails, which was hardly daunting since I usually have about fifty every time I log on. "Mrs. Day, did we do anything in class yesterday?" Um. Delete.

"Hey professor, I was sick, so yesterday was an excused absence, right?" My shoulders droop.

"Professor, I have to leave class early tomorrow. I am really sad about it though because I think we are discussing love styles, right? I really wanted to know about that." Things are looking up.

Then my eyes hit the next message. It was a student who had not been in class all week. She had emailed me the previous Sunday. Her father had called her because her mother had a seizure. She ran as fast as she could. When she got there, her mother was awake but rambling a few strange things that she did not think made sense. She took her to the ER. Within twenty-four hours, she learned that her once-healthy mother had aggressive stage 4 breast cancer.

"We are going to fight this," she said as her closing thoughts before hitting "Send." Only four days later, her mother died. Her cancer had apparently spread to her brain—she had eight tumors. Her family had no idea she was even sick. In fact, five days earlier, they had discussed the Thanksgiving menu. And then they had to force themselves to acknowledge funeral preparations.

This is our world. Like it or not, this is the world in which we live. A once-perfect and tranquil Eden became devoured by sin, and the light that God originally spoke into existence has been growing dimmer ever since. In the aftermath of sin, we have been left naked. We, who were once robed in the glory of God, are naked.

It's dark and it's cold, and our hands fumble for something to fix it. Botox? Maybe that will help us feel better about ourselves. Alcohol? Surely that bottle will warm our freezing tongues. Anxiety and depression medication. Surely these pills will make us less numb. Food? Perhaps if we just feed our bellies more rich, exotic, or succulent foods, maybe then we will be able to feel less . . . well . . . naked. And so the cycle starts and has reached astronomical rates. Combine all this with the crucial human dilemma that we are excruciatingly lonely, and you have a concoction that is enough to kill most people.

I watch a lot of prison shows. I am slightly obsessed with the ethical treatment of forgotten members of society. I used to think that there were just good and bad people, but now I think there are just broken people who make bad choices and wind up worse off than the rest of us. We are all naked. All of us. We tend to focus on the delinquents of society and point the finger at them, but we are all to blame. Our thoughts are perverse, and our words divide. Everyone is out for themselves, and many times it is hard to find examples of compassion in a world that is so cold.

Sometimes I get bogged down by the emptiness or the brokenness I see, and that's when I have to reread Genesis 1:1–3. "In the beginning God created the heavens and the earth. Now the earth was formless and empty, darkness was over the surface of the deep, and the Spirit of God was hovering over the waters. And God said, *'Let there be light,'* and there was light."

Think about the greatest sunset you have ever seen, or the most serene ocean wave. God spoke that into existence. That is how powerful God is. Just the sheer sound of His voice sends atoms into alignment. The vibration of His vocal cords is packed so full with power and energy that molecules go into a frenzy at the very command of His whisper. God speaks four words, and the laws of nature literally bend themselves to obey the curve in His syllables. He is so big that just four words bring something where there was nothing.

What scene of brilliance do you believe He could speak into your life? His voice alone is magnificent enough to bring millions of galaxies into existence. What do you think could happen when He says your name? Don't underestimate what one touch from the hand of God can do to your naked body. You are His, and that is the one thing about living in this world that makes dreaming even possible. Yes we are naked; yes, there is darkness; yes, this is not our home; but the vibrato of His voice can and will restore.

His first call to action was to bring about a light that would literally make darkness hide. Can you imagine how bright that first day in Eden must have been? I would assume that whatever we consider brightness now was nothing compared to Eden. God called for light, and darkness ran. I think it is also interesting to mention that God is often synonymous with light.

First John 1:5 says, "This is the message we have heard from him and declare to you: God is light; in him there is no darkness at all."

First Timothy 6:16 says, "Who alone is immortal and who lives in unapproachable light, whom no one has seen or can see. To him be honor and might forever. Amen."

God is light, and I believe that when He first spoke light into this world, He was also making us a promise: *where light is, there I am also.* Never forget that. If you ever think, *Surely this situation is so dark that God is nowhere to be seen,* just look toward the Son. He is still here. In the midst of a dimming world, light can still be found. Every morning when I see the sun rise, I am reminded that God is still with us. Our world is crumbling, we are naked and afraid, but He is still with us.

Satan has worked tirelessly to attack the very first words God ever spoke on this planet. But God is not a liar. What He speaks will be done. He has already given the command, "Let there be light," and so there will be light. As Satan works feverishly to destroy this globe, cling tight to the hope of restoration.

Throughout the rest of this book, my husband and I will share with you some of our personal stories. I am a communications expert, author, speaker, Christian, mother, wife, and teacher. I am also undeniably naked. My students often say to me, "Your life seems perfect." I wish I could tell my secular classroom that my God is perfect, but my life is anything but. My life is filled with regret, pain, shame, and embarrassment. I have known humiliation, and poverty; I have kissed betrayal, and heartbreak. My life is but a filthy rag sewn to worn-out skin. I, like everyone else, am trying desperately to keep it together, while the world around me seems to be falling apart.

As you go through this journey with my husband and me, I want you to keep in mind: this world is dark, but God needs you to shine bright. This world is unfair—He knows that. It is the cost of sin. It is the aftermath of nakedness. Satan wants you to give up; he wants you to feel as though God is not enough and that there are more fulfilling options than the Cross. He is a liar. John 8:44 tells us, "He was a murderer from the beginning, not holding to the truth, for there is no truth in him. When he lies, he speaks his native language, for he is a liar and the father of lies."

Satan is living in a world of blackness, and he is busy snuffing out lamps as he roves around like a roaring lion. He is a walking dead man, hoping you will become so enamored in darkness that you forget what God has promised in the very first lines of Genesis. He is hoping to infect you with darkness.

I posted on Facebook about my student, her mother, and the gloom of cancer. I said how my heart ached to see Jesus come. "This is NOT our home," I wrote.

14

My friend Candace read that status and replied, "We can do something in spite of darkness—we can pray. We can pray so hard that tiny beads of light rip through dark walls."

I agree with her. My Bible is filled with saints from before, who have achieved the impossible by claiming the glory of heaven. Joseph, a slave, became a ruler in Egypt; Moses, a runaway, divided the Red Sea; and Peter, a fisherman, walked on water. It was not by their own might that they did these things; for they, like us, were naked. *But something miraculous always happens when people grab hold of the robe of Jesus. He covers them.*

My prayer is that every person reading this book gets filled with God's unapproachable light. I am praying for you as your eyes dance across this page. I am praying because the harvest is plenty but the workers are few. I am begging God to surround you with shafts of His light so that you may never be the same. May we start a fire that blazes across this planet and brings our Savior back. May what happened in Genesis be fulfilled because we are here.

Despite our nakedness, there is one truth that we must hold on to until the evening that Jesus comes. The echo of God's voice in Eden can still be heard today. In the midst of darkness, let there be light! He is still with us. You are His light to a fallen world. May we struggle to stand in the beams of heaven. May we find purpose and meaning in life after Eden.

**Share the Naked Truth:**

1. What was the last experience you went through in which you saw God's "light" (presence) clearly in your life?

2. In what areas of your life do you feel the most naked?

3. In 140 characters, describe the most painful difference between our world and Eden. Tweet/Facebook us *@InLifeAfterEden.*

4. Or Instagram us a photo of your favorite highlighted quote from this reading.

# Adam: From Glory to Fig

But to punish and not to restore, that
is the greatest of all offenses.—Alan Paton

The twenty-first-century man is finding himself in a huge dilemma.
With negative media messages and job loss, men on a global scale are
losing their role in society. It is clear that men were created with prestige
and honor in Eden; but after Adam fell and the pair discovered themselves
naked, the males of the race have been recipients of a degenerating legacy.
Here is what Ray Williams had to say about men in his article published
in 2010:

First, we are seeing a significant shift in the nature of education and
employment trends which will have a huge impact on male identities. Boys are seriously under-achieving in public schools in the U.S.,
Canada, the U.K. and Australia, according to several recent research
studies. Men now comprise barely 40% of enrolled University and
College students and graduates. In fact, a gender education gap, in
which women are far outpacing men in terms of educational achievement, has been quietly growing in America over the past few decades.
In 2009, for instance, women will earn more degrees in higher education than men in every possible category, from bachelor's level to
Ph.D.s, according to the U.S. Department of Education. When it
comes to masters-level education, for instance, U.S. women earn 159
degrees for every 100 awarded to men. For the first time, less than

17

50% of law school graduates are men in North America.*

It is clear that leading experts are seeing this trend in the men of the twenty-first century. Williams goes on to say that women are passing men in every area of life. For the first time in this earth's history, women are taking roles of power such as principals, political figures, and church leaders. Because of this, men are finding themselves lost on a global scale.

From lack of education to job loss and depression, men are losing their identity all around the world. The side effects of these events are leaving families around the world in a state of dysfunction and could be contributing to the latest epidemic: fatherless homes.

For most of my childhood and early adult life, I was extremely apprehensive and skeptical of almost all men. I often confined myself to my own thoughts and shut the world out. I chose to box myself in and became trapped within the prison walls of my own mind. I don't think this is how I was originally created to be, or even desired to be. I fell victim to a sickness that is destroying little boys and girls everywhere as you read—children in the wake of absentee fathers.

Life after Eden is a life that I realized, quite early on, would be filled with anything but the perfect families I saw on TV. As a result of what happened that day in Eden, this world would be digesting the plagues of sin in large doses.

Before we get into all the mumble-jumble you are probably expecting, I will address any preconceived notions you might have by saying this: I am not expecting this book to change your life. That is something you will have to wrestle with personally. I am not guaranteeing that by reading this book you will automatically have a spiritual revival. That depends on whether or not you take seriously the messages conveyed throughout the pages. Honestly, with this book, the more you put in, the more you will get out. This book is a seed; what you do to cultivate it is all up to you. Your attitude, your desire, your openness to change, these are going to

* Ray Williams, "Our Male Identity Crisis: What Will Happen to Men?" *Psychology Today*, July 19, 2010, https://www.psychologytoday.com/blog/wired-success/201007/our-male-identity-crisis-what-will-happen-men.

be the door that opens your understanding for where we are in *Life After Eden*, and whether or not it leaves you with any personal obligations. I can assure you of this: I have prayed over every page.

We must discard what we have been taught by society, the media, and fairy tales about earth being the land of dreams where you should want to live forever. This is not our home, and we should not be putting permanent residence here. So charge your power drills and dust off your sledge hammer, because it's time to do a little mental demolition. Here is the catch with any kind of work involving demolition, however: you will sweat and quite possibly bleed in the process. It's OK. It means progress is happening. Don't give up.

I am not saying that is going to be easy, but the reward is well worth it. On this journey you are going to search the most secluded parts of your being and drag the skeletons out one by one, exposing them, understanding them, and finally taking a hammer to them, leaving nothing but a pile of bones. Get ready. It's time to get a little dirty, bruised, and even angry. These are all tools that will help you get the job done more effectively. The key is knowing where they fit throughout the process and how they are used as we seek reconstruction through Christ.

Anger at where we are in the world today can be the driving motor behind change, or it can be the roadblock that prevents it altogether. After all, isn't anger just another word for hurt? My wife, who teaches classes on the way we communicate emotion, always reminds me that for men, anger is the default emotion. Men don't get hurt, because hurt would make us far too vulnerable. Instead, we get angry. We don't get jealous, we don't get embarrassed, we don't feel rejected, and we don't express fear. Of course, we experience those emotions, but it is difficult for us to express them without feeling feminine. So you want to know how men deal with emotion without losing their masculinity? We default to anger.

Growing up, I had a lot of angry moments in my life. My father was a poor example of a man, though I must say that he has grown with time, and was doing the best he could with the cards he was dealt and the examples he was shown. I had to learn a lot of life's lessons the hard way, and they made me hurt, or, more accurately, angry. I was raised by my mother. I had an older and younger brother. There were many times we desperately needed the advice of a credible male. Instead we would often discover my mother trying time and time again to think like one. There was only one small problem—my mother is a woman.

Having no choice, she stepped into the double role of mother *and* father. She was wonderful and lovable, but the shoes she wore were far too big for her. She looked awkward in them. I found my mother stumbling a lot when it came to topics involving sexuality and the everyday routine of men. I'll never forget when I hit puberty and bizarre things started to happen. Hair grew in strange places and my face started to itch from all the peach fuzz accumulating on my cheekbones. Stealing a razor from my mother's bathroom drawer, I dipped it into cold water and mimicked what I had seen on television. I was fourteen years old when I discovered that warm water and soap went a long way in this surgical procedure. I also learned that not having a dad was a lot like shaving with nothing but cold water; it burned.

That was just one frustrating experience in a very lengthy list to come. Growing up without a father is one of the biggest struggles human beings are faced with in this life after Eden. It is a constant reminder that we were meant for more than a garment of fig leaves. We were meant for a life that illuminates the glory of God fully. Fatherless boys and girls can never escape this truth. They are reminded day in and day out that this life we call the American dream is anything but perfect. They have no choice but to live the American tragedy.

Growing up, one of the things that struck me the most about not having a father was not necessarily the big moments in life but the small moments that let me know something really big was missing in my life.

It was my eighth-grade graduation, and the entire class rented tuxedos for the event. My class at Battle Creek Academy had about thirteen students in it. I'll never forget getting dressed that evening. It took me an hour to figure it out. All the buttons just confused me. My mother did the best she could to help. Living on campus, I trekked over to the school feeling like a million bucks in my shiny shoes and fancy buttons.

I was the last one to arrive. When I got there, everyone was lined up to take pictures in our classroom before the ceremony. Once I found my place in the center of the group, everyone started to giggle. All the parents were laughing. And then the rest of my classmates started to squirm with laughter as well. I didn't know what was so funny, so I joined in, not wanting to be the only one not laughing. Finally, a parent gently laid his camera on a table and walked directly toward me. It was the dad of one of my classmates. Kneeling down in front of me, he started undoing my buttons one by one. You see, I had big buttons where little buttons should be, and vice versa. All the while the room erupted with "innocent" giggles. I immediately wanted to melt into nonexistence, I was so angry. No, I mean embarrassed. I wanted to scream at the top of my lungs and just tell everyone to be quiet. Everyone else had a dad to help them get ready. It just wasn't fair. To this day when I look back on that story I still feel the shame of being fatherless, abandoned, and altogether forgotten.

Things didn't get any easier as life progressed. Two years later I found myself expelled in the midst of my sophomore year—I had gotten kicked out of our little church school. I made a dumb decision, and the consequences were enormous. The word spread like wildfire about what I had done, and within a few hours I was sitting in the principal's office reaping the aftermath of my decision. My mother was hysterical. She was a teacher at the school, and I don't know if I had ever heard her cry so hard in my life up until that point.

Over the next few months I felt really alone. Staring out the window of our campus house, I watched my classmates play flag football at PE. But this is where my life changed. One of those lonely days I remember just sobbing immensely in our living room in the dead of the afternoon. All I could think about was how much I needed my dad. I needed advice. I was lost, alone, and scared. Going to a Christian school, you hear a lot about God, but that didn't mean that I had ever accepted Him into my life. To be frank, I could not have cared less about God up until then. Being at this all-time low, I decided to open my Bible, not because I had a test or a homework assignment, but because I had nowhere else to turn. With tears streaming down my cheeks, I opened my Bible and began reading the verses I had heard the most, John 3:16 and Psalm 23, all the while crying out for God to make Himself real to me. I just kept saying over and over again, "I need to feel You, I need to feel You." And in the midst of my fumbling around the pages I turned to the index in my Bible and looked up the word Father. And this is the next text I read, Romans 8:14, 15: "For as many as are led by the Spirit of God, these are sons of God. For you did not receive the spirit of bondage again to fear, but you received the Spirit of adoption by whom we cry out, Abba, Father" (NKJV).

It was in that moment that I felt a huge weight lifted off my shoulders, and the arms of God embraced me. It was that moment in my life when God became real. It was that moment when I found what I was looking for—someone to call Dad. Reflecting on this text now, it's more amazing to me. Listen to this quote by the theologian F. F. Bruce in his commentary on Romans: "The term 'adoption' . . . may have a somewhat artificial sound in our ears; but in the Roman world of the first century AD an adopted son was a son deliberately chosen by his adoptive father to perpetuate his name and inherit his estate; he was no whit inferior in status to a son born in the ordinary course of nature, and might well enjoy the father's affection more fully and reproduce the father's character more worthily."*

Do you get the power of Bruce's words? Think of it this way: in the first century A.D., if the heir to all your family's estate is your biological son, you are just hoping he is a good fit. But if your heir is your adopted son, it is because you know you have chosen the perfect fit. Today, the same principle concerning our heavenly Father is still true. He has deemed every fatherless man, woman, and child the perfect fit. God is desperate for you and wants nothing more than to restore you to your original state of life before the fall of humanity. He wants to give you a life with a hope and a future—a life that isn't naked.

God has already purchased you. The adoption papers are all filled out, and He is on His way right now to take you home. I know firsthand that at times the void of being a fatherless child is immense, but you have to hang on. Your heavenly Father is just a few blocks away. He has rented a limousine and is accompanied by heaven's finest choir. I can hear Him right now yelling to the driver, "How much longer? I can't wait to hold my child!" So take one hard, last look at those cold, rigid fig leaves you're forced to wear, and get prepared to hit "Erase" on the DVR button. For this is the final episode of *Life After Eden*. And with your Father's arrival, a new season will begin.

---

* F. F. Bruce, *Romans*, Tyndale New Testament Commentaries (Downers Grove, IL: Intervarsity Press, 1985), 167.

I have had the opportunity to read the script for the following season. I won't spoil it for you, so all I will say is this: The first episode is entitled "From Fig to Glory." It's time to gather your belongings and start marching toward the sidewalk curb, because your father can only take you home if you're patiently waiting for His arrival. Your American tragedy is in its closing scene. It's just about over. The credits will soon roll across the heavens and then the sequel will start playing. You see, this first part, titled, "From Glory to Fig" was written by the director of sin, the devil.

Here is the good thing, though. God is the editor. He gets to do the final critique. Where the devil has written the words, "eternally naked," the Editor didn't find it fitting for His children. So He inserted an element of surprise into the storyline that the devil wasn't expecting—an underdog who saves the day. In the heart of the devil's screenplay, God did the unimaginable: He took His red pen and added a new character. The scene was Calvary, the underdog was Jesus. And this, my friend, was the crossing of the t's and the dotting of the i's on your adoption paper.

*"When everything is ready, I will come and get you, so that you will always be with me where I am" (John 14:3, NLT).*

**Share the Naked Truth:**

1. If your childhood was a movie, what would it be called and why?

2. In what areas of your childhood did you feel the most naked?

3. In 140 characters describe what it means to be adopted by God. Tweet/Facebook us *@InLifeAfterEden.*

4. Or Instagram us a photo of your favorite highlighted quote from this reading.

## Day 3 — Heather

# Eve of the Fall

Well, knowledge is a fine thing, and mother Eve
thought so; but she smarted so severely for hers, that
most of her daughters have been afraid of it since.
—Abigail Adams

One of my favorite chapters to teach in my Interpersonal Communications class is the chapter on listening. As a culture, we are losing the ability to listen to one another. Listening used to be the premium in accurate communication. If you did not listen, you would be unable to know much of anything that was happening around you. There was a time when knowledge was only attained through the art of accurate listening. Hearing is passive. You can hear many things and never quite be sure what exactly you heard. Hearing happens when your ears pick up sound. It is mindless and takes zero effort to occur. However, listening is active. You have to concentrate and focus if you want to be a good listener.

One thing about listening that people often do not realize is its connection to power. We often think that in order to be a good leader you have to be the best talker. There is absolutely zero correlation to the person who first shares their thoughts on a question and the correct answer. There is a correlation, however, between listening and leadership. Great leaders are often great listeners.

Why is it so hard for us to listen to one another today? For starters, we developed means of recording. The second we were able to write and record information, the focus on accurate listening decreased. You didn't have to pay such careful attention to what people said about advice, history, family genealogy, or politics, because you could read it all later. There was a time when the only way to share family genealogy and stories was by listening and memorizing them.

Something I think is interesting is what happens when we hear repeated sounds. When my children cry in the car, I feel bad for the person in the passenger seat. If a friend is traveling with me, and my kids start crying, I often barely hear the crying. I am so used to them crying when we are in the car that my brain treats their screams as standard background noise. Our brains distinguish noises that are new, but they discount sounds that stay the same.

Sometimes I think this is what happens when we hear Bible stories. If we grew up in Christian families, stories such as Abraham and Isaac, Adam and Eve, and Jesus of Nazareth are stories that become background noise. We cease to hear them because we feel as though there's nothing new. But we cannot approach Scripture this way. How can we truly hear the subtleties and whispers of the Holy Spirit when we tune everything out? A friend of mine once said to me, "I don't know if God is too quiet or if my life is too loud."

I am not sure if, outside of the story of the Crucifixion, we can find any biblical example of a love story greater than that of Adam and Eve. Our view of marriage and male/female relationships has become so distorted that it is difficult for us to even picture the perfect person, never mind the perfect relationship. This is what they had in Eden, though. Adam and Eve are the only two people ever to walk the face of this planet who were able to experience marital intimacy the way God intended.

The marriage in Eden before the Fall was one of unimaginable unison. They experienced and shared a tenderness and respect for one another that no other relationship in the human experience can re-create.

Often when discussing biblical headship, women can get a little uncomfortable. The thought of having men lead them doesn't sit right anymore, and I don't really think we are wrong for feeling that way. Our culture is so perverted with images of male abuse and disloyalty, especially in marriages, that the idea of having a man as the head of a woman makes most women want to find a new religion.

We have to remember, though, that this new naked picture of men is not what God created in Eden. I am sure Eve would have had no issues with Adam having headship over her. Why would it be bothersome to her that Adam, who loved his wife unconditionally, would experience a type of leadership over her in the marriage relationship? It is my belief that the only reason this ideology would ruffle feathers is that we have seen so many bad examples of men and marriage. We have witnessed so many unloving husbands that the thought of the Bible expressing the importance of a man's leadership in the marriage union is scary.

We have to remember what marriage was intended for—to bring partnership and joy to one another and symbolize our relationship to Christ. Marriage was never meant to be oppressive. Susan Foh said it best when she said,

> We know only the arbitrariness, the domination, the arrogance that even the best boss/underling relationship has. But in Eden, it was different. It really was. The man and the woman knew each other as equals, both in the image of God, and thus each with a personal relationship to God. Neither doubted the worth of the other nor of him/herself. Each was to perform his/her task in a different way, the man as the head, and the woman as the helper. They operated as truly one flesh, one person. In one body, does the rib rebel against or envy the head?*

Adam loved Eve, so much so that when faced with losing her, he couldn't do it. Genesis 3:6 says, "When the woman saw that the fruit of the tree was good for food and pleasing to the eye, and also desirable for gaining wisdom, she took some and ate it. She also gave some to her husband, who was with her, and he ate it."

She's standing there, beautiful as ever. Her frame poised and elegant. Eve brings the fruit to Adam. It was rotten but looked glorious. It would spoil in her stomach but fell sweet on her tongue. She ate it. In one bite, Eve swallowed down what was left of her innocence. I am sure that Adam's

---

* Susan T. Foh, *Women and the Word of God* (Phillipsburg, NJ: Presbyterian and Reformed Publishing, 1979), 62.

eyebrows rose immediately. Suddenly, Adam felt fear. He swallows back a lump in his throat, and his eyes bulge from their sockets. Sweat starts to collect under his arms, and his heart gives birth to a new emotion—panic. If he doesn't eat the apple, Eve will probably die, and he would rather they both be lost. Adam cannot imagine life without Eve, and so without a further thought, he sinks his teeth in, and the world as they knew it was over.

Immediately Satan screams in exaltation. He flexes his muscles and grins so large that all his canine-like teeth show. He fashions himself a crown and places his body on a self-made throne. This is his world now.

God created Adam as ruler of Eden. When Satan defeated Adam, I am sure he believed he was the rightful new heir to this beautiful earth. His laughter echoed from the mountaintops, and his minions clapped their hands. All you can hear are the purrs from the slithering tongue of a slimy snake.

And in heaven? You heard . . . nothing. Harps were quiet. Singing was hushed. Laughter was silenced, and joy was crushed. Seconds passed, and then finally a sound. Like a drop of water getting larger before crashing to the ground, a tear fell from the eye of God, and its echo reverberated across all of heaven.

I can almost see an angel, maybe Gabriel, stepping forward and putting his hand across the shoulder of Jesus.

"We cannot allow them to keep living," he whispers, afraid of what Christ may be thinking. "They are sinners now," he continues slowly. "They've chosen Lucifer."

God remembers the image of Lucifer exiting heaven, taking sympathizers with him and destroying forever the holy family.

"Shall I go?" I envision another angel stepping forward. His sword is drawn. "They knew the rules," he continues. He is feeling nervous about letting the pair continue on in Eden in their new toxic state. Satan had ruined so much. He couldn't let Adam and Eve perpetuate a similar chaos. Christ had been through too much already. Suddenly, to heaven's uncomfortable gaze, Jesus walks toward the Father. The angels stand silent and shift their eyes to not intrude on their privacy. When Jesus returns, the tears are gone. The grief seems to have subsided. He calls a meeting, and all of heaven attends. He shares with them His plan for redemption and sees that He is the only one still smiling.

"Please, Father," Gabriel urges, "they've made their choice." The thought of their King being scourged by cruelty and pierced with nails seems too heavy a cost.

"What is He thinking?" the angels mumble. "This plan is far too risky."

"They are My children," Jesus answers with resolve.

"Then I'll go," says Gabriel.

"No, I'll go," says another. Soon all of heaven is in a panic. They cannot wrap their minds around what Christ is saying. How could they, in good conscience, let Him go to earth to be murdered? He is the gentlest, most loving Being they've ever known. The thought of Him suffering infuriated them. Better it be them than Jesus.

"It has to be Me," He replies, not budging. "But you will have a role. You will go to earth and watch over them. When they cry, I want you to comfort them. When they are about to make stupid choices, I want you to whisper in their ears. They are going to find themselves in dark alleys with no hope, and your wings will be the perfect size to cover them."

With hesitation, but with trust in the Savior, they nod their heads in affirmation. Where He goes, they will go; His people will be their people. Jesus explains to the heavenly host that He would vanquish sin once and for all. That the slithering serpent would be caged and destroyed. Yes, He would suffer, but the end would be worth the pain. He had to make a road toward reconciliation. Adam and Eve were His children, and Eden would never be as beautiful without them.

Verse 7 continues, "Then the eyes of both of them were opened, and they realized they were naked; so they sewed fig leaves together and made coverings for themselves."

And just like that, the once-perfect pair fell. Adam and Eve would live long enough to fully understand the consequences of their sin. They would watch and weep as they were cast out of Eden and as angels stood guard of the gates. They were banished from their home. Now they were refugees, forced to cultivate their own food and work for their shelter. The devil had told them that by eating the fruit their eyes would be opened, and that much was true. Now they knew what it meant to quiver in fear; now they knew the agony of shame. Now they experienced the pricking thorns of pain. Now they knew what it felt like to be naked. And so do we.

Earlier I talked to you about the power of listening. I would imagine that Adam and Eve experienced many long silent hours in prayer throughout life after Eden. I have been trying to spend a considerable amount of time in my prayers lately re-creating that solemn quiet. I keep asking God to tune my ears. Lately, I have been very interested in what heaven sounds like. Today, at this moment, since Eden has fallen and Satan has experienced levels of success, what does heaven sound like now?

*I think heaven sounds like flapping wings.* I can picture angels, thousands upon thousands strong, all standing at attention, waiting for the entrance of the King. I bet it sounds like whirling air in sharp silence. I bet it looks like bright lights and white robes. I bet it smells like flowers and ocean breeze. I bet it feels like awe and humility. I think in heaven there are moments when you hear nothing but angels' wings, and I'd bet it plays a melody.

*I think heaven sounds like laughter.* I have a feeling that when Jesus talks, He uses His hands. He makes vivid facial expressions and tells stories that switch in volume. I imagine that His listeners are throwing their heads back and slapping their knees. I bet He is the best storyteller, the kind of storyteller who makes you smile, and cry, and think too hard. I wonder if approaching heaven sounds like walking up the steps to your own house filled with your favorite people. You hear the distant echoes of voices that sound familiar. You hear love, you hear excitement, and you hear muffled merriment.

*I think heaven sounds like noise.* I bet it sounds like footsteps running back and forth. Like a busy room with phones ringing and people yelling. I bet it blares with the voices of people who are frantic about moving faster. I can imagine the buzz of street addresses being yelled out and names bouncing around the room.

I bet every time someone announces that a little boy is praying, the entire room of business stops. Everything grows incredibly still, and they listen to the child's stammers. With the attentive ears of a mother they hang on every word. They exchange looks with one another, smiles that cannot be contained appear, and on a few faces, eyes water.

"That is why we work so hard," one angel will whisper to the other.

Once "amen" is heard, the noise resumes and they move about, more energized than before. I bet our prayers give them energy. I think heaven sounds like noise.

*I think heaven sounds like mourning.* Psalm 56:8 says that He has collected all our tears in a bottle (NKJV). God says He keeps record of our every sorrow. I am sure that sometimes heaven sounds like broken dreams and bad choices. I bet it sounds like sudden stops and screeching brakes. I bet you can hear the songs of funerals and bad news. I bet every time an opportunity is lost for us to receive the glory they all know too well, heaven sounds like weeping. It sounds like "How could you?" and desperation. It sounds like pleading "I love you" and "Come back home!" It sounds like fists pounding on doors and whispers of a soft but firm resolve: "I will never stop loving you." He keeps record of our every sorrow. I think heaven sounds like mourning.

*I think heaven sounds like victory.* I am sure everyone sat paralyzed as they watched their King. They heard every crack of the whip. Breathless and cringing, they listened as men smacked and slapped the face of the Prince of Peace. They closed their eyes, and they heard the sweet sound of Jesus' voice finally speak at a trial in which He had stood painfully silent. "If I said something wrong, tell me what I have said, but if I spoke the truth, than why did you strike me?" His voice lingers in our ears.

In A.D. 31, on a hill at Calvary, heaven sounded like complete and utter silence. It sounded like intense agony that dug too deep—too painful to allow even a slight noise of release. They placed one set of wings over their ears to block the sound of Satan's laughter, and with the other set they covered their eyes. The sight was so gruesome and nearly unbelievable. How could the ones He came to save, the ones whose tears He had recorded, now be screaming, "Crucify him"?

For a second, heaven sounded like nails being pounded into flesh and wood being staked into a hard, cold ground. It sounded like a heart that was barely beating and sweat that turned to blood. There was a time when the once melodious rejoicing of heaven was silenced and broken. The body of their God was left mangled and beaten, hanging on a tree. Heaven sounded like the released air of one colossal, horrified gasp.

And then, after a pause so forceful it shook the ground, heaven sounded like the removal of a stone. It sounded like veins coursing and a heart beating. It sounded like silence ending and angels singing. It sounded like wings flapping and church bells ringing. It sounded like resurrection.

I think—as a matter of fact, I am certain—that in the midst of angels' wings and laughter, in the reverberations of noise and mourning, to this day, if you listen softly, you can still hear the echoes of Calvary.

Yes, I think heaven sounds like victory. Even now, in life after Eden.

*"Enter through the narrow gate. For wide is the gate and broad is the road that leads to destruction, and many enter through it. But small is the gate and narrow the road that leads to life, and only a few find it"* (Matthew 7:13, 14).

### Share the Naked Truth:

1. What is the clearest message you have ever heard from God?

2. Imagine: What do you think Adam and Eve said to God before walking out of Eden?

3. In 140 characters, describe what you think heaven sounds like. Tweet/Facebook us *@InLifeAfterEden.*

4. Or Instagram us a photo of your favorite highlighted quote from this reading.

## Day 4 — Seth

# From Adam to Ashes

It was God who gave a man's rib to a woman.
But it is man who must learn to give away his heart
and never take it back.—Richelle E. Goodrich

So I had finally found the one. I was ready to get serious. I was ready to tie the knot. I was ready to take on the responsibility of being a husband. I saved, I sweated, and I starved all in preparation for an event that would change the course of my life forever. I had the ring, I had the girl of my dreams, and I was ready to ask her to be my wife. Luckily she said yes, and as we started getting ready to plan the wedding, I decided I didn't want to wait. Why should I? She was the one. I was ready. After talking it over, we planned to get married in just two months on a cruise off the Gulf of Mexico from Clearwater, Florida. It was the best day of my life. After the honeymoon we boarded the plane to fly back home. I couldn't help but feel peace because I knew my life was coming together perfectly.

Soon after we arrived back home, my new bride sat me down and told me something that stole the peace right out of my chest—she was pregnant. I wasn't ready.

We are all ready for a lot of things in life. A promotion, furthering our education, perhaps a new house or car. Maybe you're ready to tie the knot yourself? But what you aren't ready for in this life after Eden is the next step in your relationship with Jesus Christ.

It turns out that my daughter London was the best gift that I wasn't ready to receive. I believe in this busy and fast-paced world, where wants and must-haves rule, is an indistinguishable set of hands reaching for you in the midst of seemingly pointless chaos. They are the unmistakable, nail-scarred hands of Jesus Christ. In the commotion of all the must-haves and can't-live-withouts, He is standing silent in the center of it all. He isn't screaming, nor is He condemning, He is just standing there hoping you will notice Him. Every time you push Him aside to seek the "important things" in life, you actually forfeit the essence of life itself. For Scripture tells us that "all things were created by him" (Colossians 1:16, CEB).

Not only were all things created by Him but also "created for him." The challenge is this: Will you take the time today to stop pursuing the temporary must-haves and can't-live-withouts to notice the very hands that cause you to inhale and exhale? Will you pause long enough from all the things you're ready for in this life to thank the One who gives your heart 110,000 thuds each day, and 40 million thuds each year? I believe that if you do this, you will find a blessing beyond comprehension—one that surpasses any goal you're thirsting after in this life after naked.

Having children was one my greatest fears. I was afraid of letting them down. I didn't really have a dad, so how could I be one? I was terrified of perpetuating the cycle of life after Eden. The day London was born will forever be etched in my mind as one the greatest moments I have experienced. On 11/11/11, my baby girl entered this world weighing 5lb 13oz.

And it was there in the stillness of that hospital room where I conquered one of my greatest demons. I made a commitment to my daughter and to my wife that I would not perpetuate the dysfunctional cycle of life after naked any longer. I promised my wife, who was exhausted from giving birth, that she would not become another statistic in somebody's dissertation on single mothers. I didn't care what the future would bring, I didn't care what fights we would get into, I didn't care what weight she would gain, I was going to love her the way Adam loved Eve. I was going back to Eden.

For my daughter I fell to my knees and raised her to God's throne. I asked for His anointing over her, and for Him to give me the tools I desperately needed in order to give her a clear picture of Him. In that small hospital room a new heartbeat came into the world. And each night as I tuck that little heartbeat into bed, I can be certain that another gear is broken in the vicious cycle of life after Eden. Every time my daughter or son screams "Daddy" because of another bad dream about a monster under the bed, I come running. Leaping out of bed to comfort them, painting another brush stroke in their understanding of how a heavenly Father will deal with them later in life when they are scared. I know this much about dads: when their children are in distress, daddies come running.

Every time I make the conscious decision to be a father who puts the needs of his child before his own, I clear another hurdle in this game of life after Eden. I have discovered that my life finds its greatest purpose when I stop pursuing all my must-haves and can't-live-withouts and reclaim my role as a man—a man who loves his family before himself, a man who is a lover of the daughter Eve.

Our culture has bitten into another one of the serpent's lies. It's time to spit it out. As human beings our catch phrase is, "Do what makes you happy," when in fact we were not made to be pleasers of ourselves but to be pleasers of God. I believe that if men can recapture the essence of the role delegated to us in the Garden of Eden, we will put dents in the armor of sin.

For a long time I hated my father, but now I realize that he was only mimicking the model his father had shown him. Again, with one in five children in inner cities not knowing the name of their daddies, one thing is certain: we have gone from Adam to ashes.

Phyllis Bird makes a clear reference to the story of Adam and Eve in the Garden of Eden: "The story of Adam and Eve in Genesis 2–3 does center on Adam, it does so only in treating him as 'representative of the species' the story is not about gender and sexuality, but about the 'place of humans within the created order.'"*

From her study of Genesis 2 and 3, Bird makes the distinction that the story of Adam and Eve was about the "place of humans within the created order." By going back to this place in the Bible, we will be able to better understand the role of Adam and "his place" as a man in the scheme of creation, and what this means about his relationship to Eve.

Did you know our role as men today is still the same? This is why a man may fall into a deep depression when he loses his job and is no longer able

---

* Phyllis A. Bird, "Bone of My Bone and Flesh of My Flesh," *Theology Today* 50, no. 4 (1994), 521–534.

to provide and tend to the needs of his family. He has lost his defining role as a man. This is why a man blames himself when some tragedy happens to his spouse, whether she gets raped, sick, or is just plain unhappy. His role as a man feels shaky. His role of protector of his mate feels unsteady. In other words, he has lost his "gender role."

All over the world, men are no longer able to clearly distinguish the role that was given to them by God in the Garden of Eden. I believe that as a culture of men we must strive collectively to be better spouses, fathers, and role models. We have to grab the bull by the horns and allow God to redefine us in His image, and not define God in ours. This life after naked is clear evidence that sin has run its course.

I'll never forget my sixteenth birthday. I received lots of cards in the mail, and my mother baked me one of my favorite desserts—a raspberry Jell-O cake. My caring Aunt Michelle, who lived four hours away, decided to surprise me and drive down for the occasion. I can never forget that day because she showed up driving my first car. She had purchased my first vehicle for me. It was a plum-purple 1993 Ford Ranger. I didn't care that it was purple; I loved that truck because it didn't belong to anyone else but me.

That has to be one of the nicest things anyone has ever done for me to this day. I can't tell you how excited I was to sit in the driver's seat for the first time. It was a stick shift, and I had no idea what I was doing. I spent the next several hours in the driver's seat programming my favorite radio stations and stalling out in a nearby parking lot. When I got home that evening from a long adventure of joyriding, I was whipped. I slipped under the warm covers of my bed sheets and placed my car keys on the nightstand next to where I lay.

And that's when it hit me. As I placed my keys on the dresser, I looked at the time. It was 10:00 P.M., and I had gotten everything I ever wanted that day, except the one thing I actually needed. My father never bothered to call—or even send a card. In American culture, turning sixteen is like a rite of passage into manhood. We get our driver's license and indulge in a new freedom to roam and explore. I gained my freedom that day, but I felt as though I had lost my dignity.

I couldn't help but think, *What in the world kept my dad from calling?*

That's when I pressed my face into my pillow so no one would hear me cry. Looking back on this story now, I am wise enough to realize that the reason he never called wasn't necessarily because he didn't care about me. It was beyond that. The root of the problem went much deeper.

Today, we live in a world where men never grow up, not because they don't want to but because they don't know how. Wanting to do something and being able to do something makes the difference between success and failure. I met a God who was a Savior to my manhood. My father hadn't had that intervention yet.

I believe that one of the most vital tools in bringing about the Second Coming is going to be a generation of men who can clearly define their gender role as men of God—men who don't settle for the pile of ashes this life after Eden has left us in. Instead, pushing forward in the face of adversity, they are a generation of men who fight the uphill battle with their sword in hand, a generation of men who acknowledge their fallen state and seek to change it by way of the cross of Christ.

Want to know a concept I am still struggling to accept? Men feel more fulfilled as men when they fulfill the needs of their wives. Maybe this is why you have often heard it said, "Happy wife, happy life." Or, "If mom isn't happy, no one is happy." A man's role at Creation was to be the provider, protector, and fulfiller to the needs and desires of Eve. Adam loved Eve.

Today, things have changed, and I think Adam would be disappointed. We teach boys to sleep around with as many women as they can. In fact, we tend to think it is "manly." "Boys will be boys," we mumble. Is this how God originally created the male to behave? Where did we lose the true meaning of manhood? Adam would gasp if he saw the prevailing view of many in today's male culture.

Satan has worked hard to pervert and distort the calling of men, so much so that many women now find themselves untrusting and weary of the very gender that was created to protect and cherish them. It is no wonder men in today's culture are failing to adapt in nearly every facet. Men are floundering in education, jobs, relationships, and family life. I think there is one simple concept that could start changing things back around. We must go back to Eden.

Adam loved Eve. In their relationship, the world was to get an accurate picture of Christ and the church. We need to go back to the basics; men need to love their wives more than they love themselves.

Men need to listen to women, tend to women, and care for women. We need to set our passions and desires aside, and place the needs of the daughter of Eve before our own. Eve was the crowning jewel of Creation. Life was not complete until Adam saw her. This is the key to happiness. When the needs of our spouses are met, we ultimately fulfill our own greatest desire. Our greatest role and calling as men is to love and protect Eve. It was set in motion from the beginning of time. It is a role fashioned by the hands of God, a role that, if done correctly, allows God to reveal His character through the lives of His sons. It also teaches men about selflessness and tenderness. It redefines masculinity.

Life started changing for me when I accepted that the path to a fulfilled spiritual, personal, and relational life was to first make sure I was doing everything I could to show love to my wife. You are only going to have as much peace in your life as your spouse has, and you are only going to feel security in your marriage when your wife feels secure. I really think it is how we are naturally wired. My wife and I do not have a perfect marriage. I fall short daily. But my intentions in the marriage have not changed.

The man's greatest role in this life was set in motion in the Garden of Eden, and I don't think it has changed. When we go back to this ideal image of manhood, we reveal the truth about the Redeemer. We begin gluing the pieces back together. Sin has destroyed our picture of God and of men. So many people cannot truly fathom a loving God, because they have only seen examples of unloving men. This does not do justice to God. It's time to collect the ashes of Adam.

> *"Then the Lord God made a woman from the rib he had taken*
> *out of the man, and he brought her to the man"*
> *(Genesis 2:22).*

## Share the Naked Truth:

1. What is one stereotype about men you think should change?

2. What do you think is the most beautiful aspect of the male/female relationship?

3. In 140 characters, describe one of God's characteristics you know Him to have. Tweet/Facebook us *@InLifeAfterEden.*

4. Or Instagram us a photo of your favorite highlighted quote from this reading.

# When God Says No

Faith is the bird that feels the light
and sings when the dawn is still dark.
—Rabindranath Tagore

I remember it as though it were yesterday. I had recently given birth to my daughter, and we were living in a duplex with no cable TV, Internet, or spare cash to go out on the weekends. Prior to this I had left a well-paying job with benefits to teach twelve credit hours a semester at a community college. I had done it for one year at this point because I felt as though that was what God wanted me to do. We were barely scraping by.

My husband was working full time at a job he was grateful to have but wasn't the career of his dreams. Seth desperately wanted to go back to school and finish his religion degree. But I had quit my job with benefits a few months before finding out we were pregnant. I was twenty-four, had just finished my master's degree, and wanted to begin my career as a college professor. I knew I would have to get into a PhD program, but I was hopeful that I would find a job while I worked my way through my doctoral degree. My husband put his dreams on hold to support our family financially, while I waited for my big break in the world of academia. He was going to take care of me at all costs. I think every woman should marry a man like that.

I bet Eve did. I bet when the nights were cold it was Adam who cleared the path to the house. I bet when hands were worn, Adam kept tilling the land so that the family could be fed. I bet there were many nights that

39

Adam laid his body over Eve's, simply because he knew how embarrassed she still was to be naked, and he wanted her to feel his warmth.

When I saw the phone ringing and the name on the caller ID, I froze. It was my boss. I immediately started running through my mind whether or not I had made any mistakes in my classrooms. Had a student filed a complaint? Why in the world was my boss calling my cell phone? He was my boss, not my friend, and we did not speak on my cell phone, ever. We always communicated either in person or via email. He had never called me, not once.

"My boss is calling," I said to Seth, frozen.

"Answer it," he responded, confused as to why I was so panicked by this. He didn't understand that I was a woman and my mind was immediately creating fictional and yet possible scenarios as to why he was calling me.

"Hello," I said timidly.

"Heather," he said.

"How are you? Everything OK?" I asked.

"Great! Hey, listen, the dean just called and said our department was approved to hire a three-quarter-time professor. The position comes with your own office. You'd teach the same number of classes as you are now, but I would need you to start keeping twenty-eight office hours. It is still a contract position, but your pay will more than double, and the job is yours if you want it."

"*Yes!*" I barked without even consulting my husband. I was near tears. We were struggling financially, and having my own office on the campus would bring me mountains closer to a full-time position with benefits, which meant my husband could go back to school.

"Ha-ha, great. I'll let the dean know. Oh, and Heather, there is a possibility that full-time employment may come up soon. I'd assume you'd be interested in that as well . . ." His voice trailed off.

"That assumption would be correct," I responded. I thanked him immensely and hung up.

After filling my husband in on what had just happened, I fell to the floor and prayed. I had been praying rigorously for months that something would change for us, and God would deliver my husband from this financial burden he was under. This was an answer to prayer, and I couldn't breathe. There were several contract teachers who had been teaching for many years longer than I had in that department, and my boss choosing me to fill this new opening was surely a miracle.

I started my new job about a month later, and I can still remember the feeling of pride when I walked into the communications building and saw my name on the blackboard of professors who taught in that hall. I couldn't believe this was happening. I walked over to my office. It didn't have my name on it, but I didn't care. I took a sticky note and wrote "Heather Thompson Day" in bold letters. I stuck it to my door and stood back to marvel at the sight. I set up my stapler, calendar, and some photos of my husband and our daughter, and I got to work.

Throughout the next month, things went great. I loved teaching, I was good at it, and the office hours didn't bother me at all. My boss told me that the full-time position for next year had been approved. He told me to check the Web site daily because it should be posted soon. He never said the job was mine, but I knew I was a frontrunner, barring some Ivy League grad strolling in and destroying all my dreams. I was on top of the world.

My husband and I had wanted to purchase our first home. We found a large house right next to the lake, with boat access. It was a foreclosure and it needed work, but he was a carpenter, and it was in our budget. We made an offer. The offer was accepted, and I scheduled a home inspection. The day before the home inspection, I stopped by my boss's office. He had asked me earlier in the week to update my resume and give him a copy so he could review it. I stopped in his office with my resume in hand, beaming from ear to ear. I had just turned twenty-five, was about to have a beautiful home, and the job of my dreams making more money than I had ever made in my life. My husband was going to go back to school, and finally I could support him as he had supported me.

When I entered his office, he walked around me and shut the door behind me.

"Have a seat," he said. I knew something was wrong. His typically cheerful face was downcast, his usual small talk and jokes were absent. He seemed serious.

"The board cut the new position. I had no control over it," he said. "They want to see what happens with the economy. You should be able to keep your three-quarter-time position, though. I made sure of it."

I'm sure he said other things, but my mind went blank, my legs numb, and I desperately wanted out of his office before I broke down in tears.

"Oh, that's fine! Don't worry about it," I managed to choke out. I got out of there as fast as I could and immediately walked outside to my car. I called my mother first. I don't know what it is about heartbreak, but nothing seems to calm the sting like the voice of your mother.

She told me how sorry she was, but mostly she just listened.

"It's going to be OK. Keep your faith, and keep praying. Is the home inspection tomorrow?" she asked.

The home inspection. I had forgotten. There was no way I was purchasing a home on the lake without the raise that a full-time position was going to bring me. I was going to get foreclosed on our foreclosure. I sat in my car a few moments, sobbing, before I called my husband. I didn't know how to tell him that he wasn't going to school that fall, but at the moment I just wanted to hear his voice, to have him tell me that it was going to be OK, that perhaps we could get out of the contract for the house, though we had already signed all the papers, and that God still had a plan for us.

He gave me that. He gave me kind words and let me express my anger and disappointment. He called the real estate agent for me and told her the job we were banking on had been taken away. They let us out of the deal for the house, and my husband spent the next few months adjusting to the fact that he was not going to finish his religion degree anytime soon.

God had said no to my prayers, and I was devastated and angry for a long time. Part of me was angry with Him; I thought He had let me down. I prayed, I spent time in worship, I tried hard to be a loving, devoted Christian woman, and it didn't feel as though that mattered to Him. I had dreamed of a house and a new life for my family, and instead I was met with the bitter truth—this was not Eden, and I was naked.

Months passed in this numb state, but then I got over it. We found a new house and bought it that summer. It was a lot cheaper, and I could still see the lake in the distance from my bedroom window. I continued praying for a way for my husband to go to school, which would mean I would need to get a full-time job.

That August, one week before I was to go back to my nice office, teaching the classes that I loved, I received an email from the college. My boss had stepped down from his position as head of the department. He would be retiring soon. The new chair sent me a letter, stating that the new administration would no longer need a three-quarter-time employee. I lost my raise, my new title, and even my sticky note. I was back where I started.

It felt as though someone had punched me in the stomach. Now expecting our second child, I had finally started to feel comfortable with the rejection I had suffered the previous February and the dreams that were placed on hold. I was finally feeling like me again, and with one email my income was more than cut in half. I honestly couldn't believe it. I read the letter over and over again, hoping that I would somewhere find an encrypted "just kidding."

How could God do this to us? Hadn't I already suffered enough? I was afraid to tell my husband that not only was he probably not going to be able to continue taking the two classes he was already taking in order to inch his way toward a degree, but that we were suddenly in serious financial trouble again, only this time with a mortgage and a second child in the oven.

My husband spent the next semester literally working from 7:30 A.M. till 8:00 or 9:00 P.M. every evening in order to supplement my lost income. That left him no time to take classes, and really no time to see his family. He slept and he worked.

Genesis 3:17–19 kept running through my mind every time I watched my husband destroying himself physically to keep a roof over our heads.

To Adam he said, "Because you listened to your wife and ate fruit from the tree about which I commanded you, 'You must not eat from it,'

"Cursed is the ground because of you;
through painful toil you will eat food from it
all the days of your life.
It will produce thorns and thistles for you,
and you will eat the plants of the field.
By the sweat of your brow

you will eat your food
until you return to the ground,
     since from it you were taken;
for dust you are
     and to dust you will return."


Suddenly, we experienced days when we were so poor we couldn't even put toilet paper on a credit card. I applied for food stamps, and since my husband was working so much, we were approved for eleven dollars a month. I didn't even know that they gave awards that small! They didn't understand that every dollar he was making was going toward our new mortgage, diapers, and bills. There was no money left for groceries. Apparently the data said we were not in poverty, but what is it called when I cannot afford diapers, and my husband and I are living on grilled cheese and beans?

For my daughter's first birthday, I sobbed driving home from the dollar store, because I spent every penny to buy cute paper plates and napkins for her party—I couldn't afford to get her presents. I got her plates, and I threw a small party for friends and family, pretending that our party hats were somehow symbolic of our lives. I thought I was poor in the past, but you don't know what poor is until you are going to your mother's house to borrow rolls of toilet paper and boxes of cereal.

There have been moments in my life when, no matter how bad I wanted it, wished it, or willed it, God still told me no. It hurt like you wouldn't believe, and I have tiny scars all over my heart from nights that I couldn't sleep and days when I collapsed to the floor sobbing in prayer for deliverance. Time and time again in my life, God has closed doors in my face and I couldn't understand His reasoning or see His logic. Time and time again, I have been reminded that this is life after Eden.

I gave up control of my life in 2009. In 2009 I gave God permission to take the wheel and eject me from the driver's seat. Since then, I have had many blessings, most I never saw coming. But I have also had many rejections and failures. I have been built up to be broken back down, and watched this big, bad world chew me up and spit me out.

I told God in 2009 that if He would bless my writing, I would allow Him to use my life as a display. I would be honest about my failures, my weaknesses, and my shortcomings. I would be transparent about my feelings and love for Him. I wanted Him to bless me in such a way that others would be blessed.

Here is one of the biggest lessons I finally learned to swallow in life after Eden. Our faith cannot be dependent upon God the "Yes Man." Our faith must be dependent on the fact that the Bible tells us God is good, and so we believe it. If God is good, then He will vindicate and deliver His children. The Bible tells us in Matthew 7:11, "If you, then, though you are evil, know how to give good gifts to your children, how much more will your Father in heaven give good gifts to those who ask him!"

And so in spite of the "no" answers and closed doors, I had to continue to cling to faith and remain constant in my prayers to ask God to show me the right path. In this world we will suffer, and yet we must learn to be confident that in spite of our present suffering that God has not left or forsaken us. In spite of our poverty, our sickness, our brokenness, our hurting, God has not left us and will hold us if we continue grasping at the soles of His feet and begging for mercy. Satan wants you to hear God say no and get angry and leave. The devil is hoping that you will be discouraged, forget that God is good, and run your mouth to your friends about God's disloyalty. Hold fast to your faith.

The Bible tells us in Hebrews 11:6, "Without faith it is impossible to please God, because anyone who comes to him must believe that he exists and that he rewards those who earnestly seek him." Faith is the key to the kingdom of heaven. *True faith is only accomplished by a true relationship with Christ. If our faith is weak, so is our relationship.*

Second Corinthians 5:7 says, "For we live by faith, not by sight." And 1 Peter 5:9 reminds us that we must keep faith in our hour of suffering: "Resist him [the devil], standing firm in the faith, because you know that the family of believers throughout the world is undergoing the same kind of sufferings."

I petitioned God daily for about three years for a full-time job in my chosen field. He was silent. Perhaps you have a prayer you have been bringing before His throne for the last year, or three, or ten. Or perhaps you were overcome with grief and so you gave up. Well, today, let's start new. Today, let's pray together. Prayer is one of the most crucial focuses we must embrace if we are to live life after Eden. I am committed to praying for every reader of this book, that through this devotional, we will take the first step in preparing our hearts for His return. Always remember that faith is believing without seeing. We must commit to living life after Eden even when God says no to our most heartfelt prayers. I challenge you during this journey together to continue praying in faith. Continue believing, even though you do not see.

This right here, right now, is a test, and we must endure to keep strong in our relationship and keep strong in our faith. Pray for clarity. Sometimes God will say yes, but other times God will say no. That's the sermon that many Christians do not want to preach, because we are afraid it will scare away the prospects. We are quick to display the blessings while closeting the pain. I am convinced, however, that nothing makes Satan angrier than watching a saint encircled by suffering yet still proclaiming that God is good. God wants to come back. I am a believer that He is just waiting on a generation of Christians who agree that this world is not their home. Sometimes God says no just to keep us clear that this is not our heaven. Living life after Eden means living a life by faith. We are naked, we are reaching and grasping for anything to make us feel whole. Put your hands on Jesus. We have to love God more than we love our earthly aspirations and dreams for the perfect job, house, or family.

It wasn't until I was stripped of everything that I finally came to a place in my life where I realized that jobs and finances couldn't be what defined my faith. I had to love God when I had nothing, so that I could prove to Him that I would share His blessings when I had something. Sometimes rock bottom is the best place to start building a foundation. Empty pockets and lost houses were the foundation on which I started building my true relationship with Jesus. And today, I wouldn't trade those experiences for anything. There is a purpose to the pressure, and yours is just around the corner.

As for me, I went three years without full-time employment and with student loan debt piled to the ceiling. In that three years, my mother suggested that I start traveling and speaking in churches. I had previously published four books. I had never spoken before, unless it was in front of my students. I sent out letters, and in that first year I spoke at thirty churches. By the second year, I didn't send out a single letter and was still invited and flown all over the country to speak at universities, churches, camp meetings, and events.

After three years, the college I had contracted for was looking to hire someone full time, and I was the top candidate. But, had I not been home, and had I not lost my job, I would have never become an inspirational speaker. The very loss I was so angry at God for causing is actually what propelled me to discover my greatest gift and passion in life—ministry. I always swore the only thing I wanted in life was to be a professor. Now, I still love teaching, but visiting areas I would never have dreamed of, sharing my love of Christ and what He has done for me, has easily become my greatest joy. I get to travel once or twice a month telling people about my Savior. Right now, at this moment, I would go through three more years of unemployment all over again if God would give me what He has given me today.

I was able to claim the promise, because I was faithful through the process. Sometimes God says no. Today, I am as nostalgic for His nos as I am for His yeses. *Both roads lead to the same destination when we stay faithful in spite of what we don't understand.* Remember, faith is not believing because we see it. It's believing even when what God says doesn't make any sense. God has a promise for you. Stay faithful through the process.

Now faith is confidence in what we hope for and assurance about what we do not see. This is what the ancients were commended for.

By faith we understand that the universe was formed at God's command, so that what is seen was not made out of what was visible.

By faith Abel brought God a better offering than Cain did. By faith he was commended as righteous, when God spoke well of his offerings. And by faith Abel still speaks, even though he is dead.

By faith Enoch was taken from this life, so that he did not experience death: "He could not be found, because God had taken him away." For before he was taken, he was commended as one who pleased God. And without faith it is impossible to please God, because anyone who comes to him must believe that he exists and that he rewards those who earnestly seek him.

By faith Noah, when warned about things not yet seen, in holy fear built an ark to save his family. By his faith he condemned the world and became heir of the righteousness that is in keeping with faith.

By faith Abraham, when called to go to a place he would later receive as his inheritance, obeyed and went, even though he did not know where he was going. By faith he made his home in the promised land like a stranger in a foreign country; he lived in tents, as did Isaac and Jacob, who were heirs with him of the same promise. For he was looking forward to the city with foundations, whose architect and builder is God. And by faith even Sarah, who was past childbearing age, was enabled to bear children because she considered him faithful who had made the promise. And so from this one man, and he as good as dead, came descendants as numerous as the stars in the sky and as countless as the sand on the seashore.

All these people were still living by faith when they died. They did not receive the things promised; they only saw them and welcomed them from a distance, admitting that they were foreigners and strangers on earth. People who say such things show that they are looking for a country of their own. If they had been thinking of the country they had left, they would have had opportunity to return. Instead, they were longing for a better country—a heavenly one. Therefore God is not ashamed to be called their God, for he has prepared a city for them.

By faith Abraham, when God tested him, offered Isaac as a sacrifice. He who had embraced the promises was about to sacrifice his one and only son, even though God had said to him, "It is through Isaac that your offspring will be reckoned." Abraham reasoned that God could even raise the dead, and so in a manner of speaking he did receive Isaac back from death.

By faith Isaac blessed Jacob and Esau in regard to their future.

By faith Jacob, when he was dying, blessed each of Joseph's sons, and worshiped as he leaned on the top of his staff.

By faith Joseph, when his end was near, spoke about the exodus of the Israelites from Egypt and gave instructions concerning the burial of his bones.

By faith Moses' parents hid him for three months after he was born, because they saw he was no ordinary child, and they were not afraid of the king's edict.

By faith Moses, when he had grown up, refused to be known as the son of Pharaoh's daughter. He chose to be mistreated along with the people of God rather than to enjoy the fleeting pleasures of sin. He regarded disgrace for the sake of Christ as of greater value than the treasures of Egypt, because he was looking ahead to his reward. By faith he left Egypt, not fearing the king's anger; he persevered because he saw him who is invisible. By faith he kept the Passover and the application of blood, so that the destroyer of the firstborn would not touch the firstborn of Israel.

By faith the people passed through the Red Sea as on dry land; but when the Egyptians tried to do so, they were drowned.

By faith the walls of Jericho fell, after the army had marched around them for seven days.

By faith the prostitute Rahab, because she welcomed the spies, was not killed with those who were disobedient.

And what more shall I say? I do not have time to tell about Gideon, Barak, Samson and Jephthah, about David and Samuel and the prophets, who through faith conquered kingdoms, administered justice, and gained what was promised; who shut the mouths of lions, quenched the fury of the flames, and escaped the edge of the sword; whose weakness was turned to strength; and who became powerful in battle and routed foreign armies. Women received back their dead, raised to life again. There were others who were tortured, refusing to be released so that they might gain an even better resurrection. Some faced jeers and flogging, and even chains and imprisonment. They were put to death by stoning; they were sawed in two; they were killed by the sword. They went about in sheepskins and goatskins, destitute, persecuted and mistreated—the world was not worthy of them. They wandered in deserts and mountains, living in caves and in holes in the ground.

*"These were all commended for their faith, yet none of them received what had been promised, since God had planned something better for us so that only together with us would they be made perfect" (Hebrews 11:1–40).*

## Share the Naked Truth:

1. Describe a prayer that God said no to.

2. Do you think God has said "no" or "not right now"? What may be reasons that God has not given you the answer you are looking for?

3. In 140 characters, name part of your life you are going to completely give over to God. Tweet/Facebook us *@InLifeAfterEden.*

4. Or Instagram us a photo of your favorite highlighted quote from this reading.

## Day 6 — Seth

# Caskets and Thorns

God is most glorified in us when we are
most satisfied in Him.—John Piper

God placed the tree of life in the center of the Garden of Eden to sustain Adam and Eve. It was through their partaking of the fruit that Adam and Eve were kept alive. They thrived on the nutrients that the fruit produced. Have you ever wondered why God made Adam and Eve with this need for food in the first place? In a perfect world without sin it seems unnecessary, doesn't it? Surely they could eat from the tree of life one time and be sustained eternally. Why make them with a craving for food?

Perhaps God created them with an appetite because their need for food (the need to be physically sustained) would give them a mental reminder. Maybe God's provision of the fruit was a proclamation to them of His role as Creator. It certainly would have been a constant reminder to Adam that God, the Creator of the tree, was also the Supplier of life. Through his hunger Adam was continually reminded of the roles established by God. The Garden relied on Adam, and when he ate the fruit, it reminded him that he relied on God.

Today, many things have changed in this life after Eden. Our once-perfect world was swallowed whole by a serpent. Now we have death, fear, shame, blame, and pain. We are a far cry from Eden, but God has left us with one tiny reminder—hunger. Our appetites have never been more ravenous. In our lives, it may seem as though everyone relies on us. Just like Adam, we may find ourselves naked and juggling a lot of responsibilities.

You may have a lot of people in this world who are answering to you, but always remember that you answer to God.

Hunger was a part of our once-perfect Eden, and it is still a part of our imperfect earth. We are just as reliant upon God now as we were then. Want to know the first step toward restoration? We must recognize this one ultimate truth: we need God to satisfy our needs. I don't know about you, but I've never been so hungry.

In this ravenous world where appetite is a reminder to eat and live, 842 million people are desperately hungry right now as you read this. They aren't suffering because of incurable diseases or war. They are plagued with starvation. I have faced poverty in my life, but I have always been able to open my cupboard and find something to feed my children.

After the fall in Eden God spoke these words in Genesis 3:19: "In the sweat of your face you shall eat bread till you return to the ground, for out of it you were taken; for dust you are, and to dust you shall return" (NKJV).

Ever wonder why we can't have reward without hard work? You want to make a lot of money, you have to go to school. You want to make the basketball team, you have to work intensely in practice. You want to get the girl, you have to watch chick flicks and have heart-to-hearts. Nothing is free. Everything in this life that is worth having requires hard work to attain. Since the Fall, humanity was given a pronouncement of judgment: achievement comes through toil. You will not be able to even take a bite of food without breaking a sweat to get it.

Want to know a correlation to crime? Unemployment. Apparently when the descendants of Adam are not working, they are more likely to engage in deviant behavior. You develop character through the sweat of your brow and working hard to get what you need. God knew this. He knew what sin would do, and how idle hands would lead to poor character, especially in men. So God, in His judgment, also provides fallen men with a blessing.

Scripture goes on to say, "So He drove out the man; and He placed cherubim at the east of the garden of Eden, and a flaming sword which turned every way, to guard the way to the tree of life" (verse 24, NKJV). To God this was ultimate torture. I can only imagine the mix of emotions

God experienced that day as He led them from the garden, away from a place of safety and refuge, to what would be consequently their death. This was not an unfair punishment from God, for He had explicitly told Adam, "Of the tree of the knowledge of good and evil you shall not eat, for in the day that you eat of it you shall surely die" (Genesis 2:17, NKJV).

So here we are, thousands of years later. Dwarfed in stature and intelligence. Stumbling around like blind sheep. Willing to try anything to escape the curse of mortality. Women around the world spend millions each year investing in anti-aging products. Men scrub their scalps with toxic chemicals, transforming their hair to a more desirable shade. Everyone wants to live forever, and no one wants to get old.

Lather, oil, and rinse as much as you want. The stone above your skeleton will have the last word. There is no magic cream for this one. At the end of the day, when the makeup comes off and the hair is rinsed, the mirror reminds us that we are only fooling ourselves. Every time we slip into the seat of our car and buckle up, we are hoping this will preserve our life. And at night we click our deadbolts, thinking that this will be our safety as we sleep. All in an attempt to preserve our life.

The sin of Adam and Eve affected everything. Genesis 3:18 says, "Both thorns and thistles it shall bring forth for you."

Valentine's Day is one of the most ironic holidays we celebrate. We buy roses by the dozen, giving cherished loved ones a visible expression of our undying love. In reality we did nothing more than present our loved ones with the reminder that our love will certainly die. No wonder that graveyards are littered with roses. After all, the thorn is the symbol of our fall.

I often wonder what Adam felt the first time he pricked his finger while holding a flower. I bet he cried. I bet he watched a tiny dot of blood begin to pool on his skin, while grabbing his side. I wonder if flowers were still beautiful in his eyes? It must have been agony seeing innocence woven so tightly to misery. This was the world that Adam woke up to every morning in life after Eden.

November 18, 2004, was the day that my oldest brother died from cancer. It was the first time that the pronouncement in Genesis burst through my everyday life. It ripped through the seams of my existence. I was seventeen years old—too young to come face to face with the meaning of God's words, "For dust you are, and to dust you shall return."

When Heather and I started dating, she encouraged me to start writing letters to my brother during a variety of different life moments. And so *Letters to Tyler* began. When we had a good date and I wanted someone to tell, I sat down and wrote Tyler. When we got married, when we had our daughter, our son, when I had a good day or a bad day, whenever a cool breeze brought me a memory, I wrote. If you would indulge me, I thought this would be a fitting place to share with you one of my letters:

February 25, 2011

Dear Tyler,

It has been six years since you passed away, and at unannounced moments the sting of your death becomes so alive, so vivid. It's as if someone has grabbed your death by the horns and shaken it viciously in front of my face in an attempt to bring color to the already black-and-white memories of you that linger in my mind. Tyler, today was one of those moments. It was a profound moment in my life as I came to the realization that the wound from your death will never completely heal.

I recently visited home and walked past your picture hanging in the hallway. I stood there speechless, being lured in by the portrait of you casting a confident smile as you stared back at me as if to say, "I am a warrior who has earned his seat in the game of life."

Your strong poise screams victory, for you had been burdened with cancer three times previously and endured painful surgeries, chemo, and radiation. You were my hero, triumphing in every battle you ever fought, leaving your enemies powerless over you, unable to feed on your flesh and bone any longer.

The scars concealed on your back testified of your valor better than any pen ever could. Tyler, you truly were a magnificent warrior to watch, few could ever fill the shoes you wore as you rode with your head held high into every fight, claiming the victory in the end. What more could be said of you and your commitment to your precious family by not giving up when the odds were stacked against you? You were the bravest man I ever met. Many days I would come home frustrated with the toils of life until my mind was able to take hold of reality again by allowing your struggles to measure the insignificance of my own. You were invincible to me! A guide revealing that hardship chooses its victims without cause and reason, or at least it might appear that way.

It's hard to think that cancer was still lying deep within your cells waiting to strike once more. This time being much more aggressive in its warcraft, taking swift blows to your nervous system and vital organs, leaving you defenseless as it crept in and stole your heartbeat. You were so frail in that final moment before you drifted into a deep sleep that could only be awakened by your heavenly Father's voice.

I now understand it will not be until Jesus returns and I am reunited with you once more that I will find complete shelter from the storm of your sickness and eventual death. I must press forward anyway, doing everything in my power not to be overtaken by the enormity of the wound that's been left. I must constantly be seeking resources that will aid me till His second coming, which is why I am writing these letters to you, Tyler. Unleashing my emotions on paper and allowing each letter to act as some form of temporary refuge until Jesus calms the storm for good will hopefully get me through.

As I gazed into those blue eyes hanging in the hallway I was confronted with a new revelation. That we're all frail and no one is exempt from affliction. Even the strongest warriors are subject to death. For those of us who are still fighting, the final outcome hasn't been determined. Will we choose to have a faith like yours, holding firm to the hand of God before our earthly journey ends, knowing that we will live once more? That our reason for existing in the first place was to bring glory and honor to God even if it means being faithful to Him through death? Or will we die in fear, all the while trying to understand the purpose of life?

Your death has left me changed, certainly for the worse, and yet somehow for the better. You have exemplified the picture of a Christian warrior, Tyler, and behind you I will march into battle, following your example I too will choose to marry my King . . . for richer or poorer, in sickness or in health, and not even in death will I let us part.

Till we meet again,

Seth

*"And the dust returns to the ground it came from, and the spirit returns to God who gave it."—Ecclesiastes 12:7*

## Share the Naked Truth:

1. How has the death of a LOVED one changed you?

2. What do you think is the purpose of life?

3. In 140 characters, describe one person you cannot wait to see again in heaven. Tweet/Facebook us *@InLifeAfterEden.*

4. Or Instagram us a photo of your favorite highlighted quote from this reading.

### Day 7 — Heather

# Making Room

The world has the habit of making room for
the man whose words and actions show that he
knows where he is going.—Napoleon Hill

About thirty minutes before my daughter is supposed to be in bed, I tell her it is bedtime. She asks if she can stay up a little bit longer. I shrug my shoulders and tell her that if she cuddles close to Mommy, she can stay up for thirty more minutes. Every time there is this bright look in her wide blue eyes. Her lips curl, and she scoots into me. She thinks she has won, and so do I.

When I stand to carry her to her room, she clings tightly to my neck. "I don't want to go to bed, Mommy!" she groans. She asks to bring a doll to sleep with her, and she looks over at a slew of blond-haired, blue-eyed, plastic beauties. She reaches down and selects the only brown one.

"She looks like Mommy," she tells me.

In reality I look nothing like Dora the Explorer, but our brown eyes and matching hair perform a good substitute during sleepy nights when she needs reassurance. I push back the covers a bit and form a tight cocoon around her.

"Let's ask Jesus to keep us safe tonight," I whisper while running my fingers through her dirty-blond hair.

"And keep brother safe," she answers like clockwork. Every night I say the same thing, and every time she inserts a request in behalf of her brother, whose snores carry across the room. He's gone to bed in what feels like hours ago, and there was no exchange between the two of us about thirty extra minutes. Shortly after 6:00 P.M., with a belly full of dinner,

57

my son requests to be excused to his crib. He grabs his blanket and curls into it without casting me a second glance. In fact he rolls his body in the complete opposite direction of me. I think it is his way of saying, "Turn the lights off on your way out."

We say my daughter's prayers, and the blue of her eyes sparkles in the light of the moon seeping in through her window. She is beautiful; my precious Caucasian baby. Everyone smiles when I walk by with London at my side. Their lips curl as if to say, "She's so adorable," and then I feel their eyes cast a second look as they question whether or not she is actually mine. Sometimes I get angry if my friends with white skin are holding hands with London while we are out to eat. I know all the strangers assume she is theirs. No one would ever guess that her mother is actually Dora the Explorer.

She tilts her head to secure my stare. "I can't sleep without you," she sighs.

She pushes her body as close as she can to the wall and pats the bed at her right. She is making room for me. It is a small gesture, but it packs a punch. Sometimes I tell her no. I tell her that Mommy is going into her own bed. Other times, I squeeze my body onto her tiny toddler bed and pray the legs don't crack. We lie there snuggled up to one another, and she puts her arm around my head. She wants to grab hold of me so that even if she falls asleep, my movement will disturb her and she can request more time. Trust me, I am not guessing on this one. My child booby-traps me regularly.

There is a very valuable lesson that I have learned from my two-year-old daughter. Caring for and loving another human being so intensely has taught me about what it means to live life naked while clinging to Christ. In fact, children in some ways are the greatest piece of joy in an otherwise dreary world. My home in the evenings, while the kids argue about who gets to help me do what with dinner preparations, is the closest to Eden I think I can get. My husband pretending to be a monster and chasing them around the house, my dog jumping and barking and pretending to be one of the kids, are all moments and memories that warm my heart. My daughter has changed me for the better in many ways, but there is one lesson anyone can use—whether you have a child or not. So here it is, are you ready? If you want someone to be close to you, make room for them.

## Making Room

My daughter's attempt to lure me into her toddler bed has been going on for nearly a year, and so I am not sure why the other night it struck me so profoundly. But it did. I realized that on most nights, had she not made room for me, I would not have joined her. I would have tucked her in, led her in prayer, and then quietly stepped out. I don't make it a habit of crawling into her bed at night. She gets her fair share of snuggles, but once its nighttime, I am ready to snuggle my husband. On most nights I am ready for my kids to go to bed, and yet there are evenings when I find myself pressed up against her tiny bedframe with a small arm grabbing hold of my head. Very rarely am I there because I had planned to be there, *but my plans change simply because she has made room for me.*

Sometimes we ask God to intervene in our lives. We want big missions and large roles. We want to be commanders of a Christian army; to write bestsellers or hold a Bible study that runs out of seating. These are the things we want to do with Him and are bitter when some of our prayers go unanswered. We are saying all the right things; we have good intentions. Why are things not panning out the way we planned? In my own life, and through the help of my two-year-old, I have realized this: *if you want God to squeeze His big presence into your tiny space, you have to make room for Him.* It's simple, yet profound.

Far too often, our words say one thing but the heart says another. We ask Him to come into our lives, but we don't actually make room for Him. We hold tight to sin; we fill our beds with plastic dolls and convince ourselves they resemble Him. And then we don't understand why He won't crawl in with us. We lie sprawled out, legs dangling over the edge, taking up as much room as possible, because it is important that we remain comfortable. After all, life is about us, isn't it? That is how we ended up naked, isn't it? Satan thought God wasn't recognizing how important his role should be; Eve thought God was holding out on her; Adam couldn't bear an Eden without Eve. And so we continue the sin cycle, putting ourselves before God. We lie sprawled out in our lives, because that is how we are most comfortable, and want God to figure out where He can slip in.

I would venture to say that the sin God hates the most is self-focus. In fact, a pastor friend of mine said in a sermon, "When Satan cannot get us trapped in sin, he gets us trapped in self." It is the desire for self-promotion, self-exaltation, self-pleasure, and self-fulfillment that leads us to continually put ourselves as the number-one benefactors in our earthly relationships and spiritual ones also. Remember, it was love of self that caused Satan's rebellion. We love ourselves so much that it makes sin look less sinful if it appears to benefit self. We have affairs because we can't "help" ourselves. We refuse to work low-respect jobs because of how we worry people will perceive us. We are lonely and single and justify losing ourselves in pornography because our self needs to be gratified. We are slaves to ourselves, and it all started in Eden.

C. S. Lewis once discussed how ironic it is that Christians have such a hard time with loving the sinner but hating the sin—we seem to do so well with it as long as the sinner is us.

> For a long time I used to think this a silly, straw-splitting distinction: how could you hate what a man did and not hate the man? But years later it occurred to me that there was one man to whom I had been doing this all my life—namely myself. . . . In fact the very reason why I hated the things was that I loved the man. Just because I loved myself, I was sorry to find that I was the sort of man who did those things. Consequently, Christianity does not want us to reduce by one atom the hatred we feel for cruelty and treachery. . . . But it does want us to hate them in the same way in which we hate things in ourselves: being sorry that the man should have done such things, and hoping, if it is anyway possible, that somehow, sometime, somewhere he can be cured and made human again.*

Here is what I think has been a life-changing discovery for me in life after Eden—realizing that life isn't about me, and it isn't about you either. Part of living life naked is dying to ourselves and becoming alive only in Christ. If it isn't His will, it doesn't sparkle anymore. We want what He wants, and we move where He moves. The one prayer I have been repeating to God since the first time I read the Bible through for myself is found in Ruth 1:16. "Where you go I will go, and where you stay I will

---

* C. S. Lewis, *Mere Christianity*, rev. ed. (San Francisco: HarperSanFrancisco, 2009), 117.

stay. Your people will be my people and your God my God." At least once a week I end one of my worship sessions with this prayer while I ask God to give me the heart of Ruth.

If you want God to swarm you with His presence, then you have to make room for Him; and we do that best by dying to self and living for Him. Clear out the plastic that has been cluttering your thoughts and grab tight to His neck. Pull back the covers that have blinded you, and make yourself as small as possible. We were called to suffer with Jesus, and yet the average Christian just wants to be comfortable. Surely we have missed something! In order for Him to become great, we must become less. If you want Him to lay His life-breathing body over your dying naked one, make room for Him—stop saying what you want Him to do and scoot over.

I like to think that when we do this, His presence is so big and carries so much weight that it explodes our tiny bedframe. His plans for you are greater than your plans for yourself. So think thin, and make room for Him.

*"Where you go I will go, and where you stay I will stay"*
*(Ruth 1:16).*

## Share the Naked Truth:

1. Have you truly made room for God?

2. Is there any area of your life you are afraid to let God have?

3. In 140 characters, write a prayer to God of a sacrifice you will make in order to refocus on Him. Tweet/Facebook us *@InLifeAfterEden.*

4. Or Instagram us a photo of your favorite highlighted quote from this reading.

## Day 8 — Seth

# Divide and Conquer

So do not fear, for I am with you; do not be dismayed,
for I am your God. I will strengthen you and help you;
I will uphold you with my righteous right hand
(Isaiah 41:10).

I've enjoyed action movies my entire life. I dreamed of someday having the courage like those iconic movie-star heroes in their epic roles that leave any young boy pumped full of adrenaline by the time the ending credits scroll across the screen—heroes like Rambo—in their last-ditch effort to save the girl and stomp out the enemy. Though I am an adult now, inside I am still that little boy who wants to be something great. I still get fired up after an action movie and drool over the martial-arts skills of my childhood celebrities. There is just something so captivating when you see a person conquer an entire slew of men with nothing more than his wit and muscles.

I don't believe that I am alone in my desire. I am convinced that at the core of the human race God created this innate longing inside of us to strive for great things. Doubtful? Just look at the way technology has exploded in the last century. From horse to car to spaceship. Inside of our body is a complex and wonderfully put-together machine. We are constantly seeking ways to improve and overcome the failures of yesterday. Research has begun peeling back the science to how this phenomenon occurs. Studies show that when it comes to overcoming obstacles and achieving goals, the power resides within the mind.

# Divide and Conquer

Daniel Goleman, an author, psychologist, and science journalist, writes, "Optimism—at least reasonable optimism—can pay dividends as wide-ranging as health, longevity, job success and higher scores on achievement tests."*

That means optimism even when circumstances are challenging. James 1:12 says, "Blessed is the one who perseveres under trial because, having stood the test, that person will receive the crown of life that the Lord has promised to those who love him." The power to succeed in life and face your problems head-on is the ability to stand still when your legs tell you to run. Your childhood dream of being someone great is a battle of the mind. To be an overcomer and not be overcome is a desire to let the reward outweigh the risk. Beyond circumstance. The win comes from the mental ability to make a choice.

Michael Jordan, the greatest basketball player of all time, knows the discipline of overcoming well. In the 1997 championship game 5, he became extremely ill, suffering a fever of 103 degrees. No one would have blamed Jordan if he decided to sit this one out. After all, his circumstance rendered him sicker than a dog. Here is the catch, though. He didn't stop playing. In fact, he persevered in the midst of his biggest trial. He wasn't overcome but became an overcomer. His mind-set of perseverance despite circumstances was his greatest tool to achieving success.

Not only did he continue playing the game, Michael Jordan made the tiebreaking three-pointer against the Utah Jazz, giving the victory to the Chicago Bulls. Jordan said afterward, "That was probably the most difficult thing I've ever done. I almost played myself into passing out just to win a basketball game." That moment was defining to the rest of his career. Later he said, "If we had lost, I would have been devastated." Circumstance 0; Jordan 1. This is the classroom where perseverance and determination are learned, where the lesson of conquering is acquired.

For Jordan, stopping and contemplating the decision to stand and face his grim situation might have ended the game, but he chose to put in his mind in a place of perseverance, one that would succeed despite

---

* Daniel Goleman, "Research Affirms Power of Positive Thinking," *New York Times*, February 3, 1987, http://www.nytimes.com/1987/02/03/science/research-affirms-power-of-positive-thinking.html?pagewanted=all.

circumstance—a mode of positive thinking. In this life after Eden, we have become so deprived from this necessary evil. We find every excuse under the sun for why we haven't done what we have always wanted to.

I can't tell you how many adults I've heard say, "Well, I took two years of college before_____." You fill in the blank. God's reply: "That was ten years ago; what's stopping you now?" If there is one thing that I've learned about God, it's that His understanding of time is much different than ours. We look at time in terms of minutes, days, and years. He just sees what we've done with it. The portal to success will never come from dwelling on the failures of yesterday. Instead, let the choice of positive thinking determine where your perseverance will lead you tomorrow.

This generation has become a nation of spoon-fed prosperity. If it's not inherited and can't be Googled, then guess what? I don't want it. And this lifestyle of instant gratification coincides with a mind-set that lacks the discipline of perseverance. Maybe this, in part, plays into the staggering statistics of jobless and depressed America in this life after Eden.

Christopher Reeve once said, "What makes Superman a hero is not that he has power, but that he has the wisdom and the maturity to use the power wisely." Guess what? Whether life has handed you a bag of peaches or the pit, it doesn't mean circumstances have to dictate your future. What you do with that pit does. So persevere in spite of your short hand in life. How? You take that pit and bury it. You don't dwell on it, you nurture it. You take it and transform it into something beautiful. You do this by watering it. Day in and day out. That is what perseverance looks like in motion. Despite the world's lackluster attitude or your unfavorable circumstance—you never give up! For the Christian, failure doesn't exist, because failure only lives where doubt is allowed to dictate.

God isn't a genie. He doesn't show up if you simply rub Him once and spew your wish. He is your Father. He operates most efficiently through a relationship. His desire is to restore you to a better, stronger self; one that reflects humanity before the fall in Eden, that hungers and thirsts for success. My personal suggestion: give Him your pit. Let perseverance guide your relationship with your Father. Let God do the transforming for you. Your job? Never stop seeking Him—pit or peaches.

The truth is that the childhood dream of overcoming and conquering is instilled in each of us by our heavenly Father. It can only grow where there is heavenly cultivating. I believe that inside us all, there is a still small voice that whispers to us, "You were meant for more." Now perhaps you and I won't ever be a big shot in Hollywood, or ever take down a hundred men with nothing more than our human strength, but I do believe we all have battles that we must overcome.

And if I can be frank with you, they aren't something dreamed up by the likes of Spielberg or Warner Brothers. They are battles that oftentimes go unnoticed, they are battles that strike fear into the heart of every human being. It's losing your job, crashing your only car, listening to the doctor provide a diagnosis, or losing a loved one far too young. These are the real battles that make heroes of war. These are the stripes of the naked.

So what do we do with moments that say, "You'll never be good enough"? We learn the valuable lesson of perseverance. We give our problems to God and allow Him to do the dividing and conquering for us.

In the Bible we find the great leader Moses confronted with yet another huge obstacle. It seems as though this might be the last time we see the face of God's anointed servant. As he led the Israelites through the exhausting desert heat, we find Moses and his crew face to face with what seems to be a dead end. The Red Sea with its mighty waves sweeps water over the sandaled toes of Moses, as if to say to, "Na-na na-na, you'll never get out of this one," and then returns from whence it came. Everyone around him loses their faith and starts to complain, saying, "Because there were no graves in Egypt, have you taken us away to die in the wilderness?" (Exodus 14:11, NKJV).

Not only does Moses hear the stampede of Pharaoh's chariots rumbling in the distance, but he now has lost favor with the very ones he risked his life to save. Seems like an uninviting circumstance, doesn't it. I can't help but think how easy it would have been to just give up. To throw in the towel and admit defeat. Come on! It's only logical. Right? Who could have blamed him? As you may already know, that's not how the story ends. Moses sizes up the situation and sees there is a grim chance of making it out alive. The next words out of Moses's mouth shock every Israelite man, woman, and child.

He cries out, "Stand still, and see the salvation of the LORD" (verse 13,

NKJV). What? Has he lost his mind? They are just moments away from death. And he commands them to stand still? Any rational person would run for their life. Flee to any rock, tree, or nearby cave hoping they might be spared from the wrath of Pharaoh. Has he lost touch with reality? Someone needs to tug on his beard and wake him from his delusion. I can picture a mother in the front of the fearing crowd, clasping her baby in her arms.

Continuing on, he commands the Israelites, "Hold your peace" (verse 14, NKJV). I can just imagine the two-million-plus Israelites rumbling with anger at the request of their leader. Until the waters parted. Imagine the faces of everyone who was vomiting their nasty words at Moses when he raised his staff to the heavens and commanded the Red Sea to part. Everyone probably just stood there in disbelief as the water began to separate.

My favorite part of this scripture is not the fact that God parted the sea. It's the fact that we have access to the same God as Moses did, which means we can divide and conquer in our battles just as Moses did. There was nothing magical about Moses or his staff. It was the God in whom he chose to live.

I believe that story exists because Moses had made the conscious choice to place his life in the hands of God long before this circumstance ever occurred. That's what gave him the strength to succeed when it all went down. As Christians we are instructed by God to "stand still." Everyone wants to "see the salvation of the Lord," but few make the commitment to stand in the presence of God regardless of circumstance.

So here is the challenge. Stop looking at the Red Sea in your life and admitting defeat before you have raised your staff. In order for God to work in your life, you must learn to divide and conquer through His strength, not yours. You must never forget the words of Moses: "The Lord will fight for you, and you shall maintain your peace." That's it—the secret recipe that kept Moses one step ahead of every obstacle he faced. It was learning to divide and conquer, and that meant sizing up the situation and giving it to God. Let God fight for you, let His strength be your strength and His victory be your victory. It all starts by dividing and conquering. And in the life of a Christian that means, "Stand still, and see the salvation of the Lord."

For every little boy who dreams of being a superhero, this is the anecdote that transforms his dream into reality. So "hold your peace" this day and watch as God does a mighty work through you. Don't settle for average, when God is commanding you to divide and conquer. Don't worry about how it's going to happen, just know it will. This is how Moses succeeded time and time again in the face of his adversaries. And this is how you will triumph in the midst of your own. You were meant for more. And the only way you will conquer your battles is by raising your staff daily to heaven, acknowledging that in order to claim victory over this life, you must first lay it down in surrender.

I read a quote once by Andrew Murray, a South African pastor, who said, "God is ready to assume full responsibility for the life wholly yielded to Him." Moses's life was living proof of this. Today, God wants to take full responsibility for your life as well. He is begging you to stop running and just be still. Maybe your walk with God thus far has been from the viewpoint of the Israelites, never seeing the forest through the trees. Spewing one grumble after another. I challenge you to remove yourself from this way of thinking. It's time to realize that you are meant to live for more. You were born to divide and conquer, so raise your staff to the One who is able to overcome.

*"The Lord will fight for you, and you shall hold your peace" (Exodus 14:14, NKJV).*

## Share the Naked Truth:

1. Who is your favorite biblical hero?

2. Is there an area of your life where you think God just wants you to be still?

3. In 140 characters, explain the last time you saw God vividly in your life. Tweet/Facebook us *@InLifeAfterEden*.

4. Or Instagram us a photo of your favorite highlighted quote from this reading.

## Day 9 — Heather

# What Is Truth?

Don't bend; don't water it down; don't try to make it
logical; don't edit your own soul according to the fashion.
Rather, follow your most intense obsessions mercilessly.
—Anne Rice

I once attended a series of messages about the table of truth on which we base our Christianity, presented by David Asscherick. On the first night he presented a "truth" I felt I had forgotten in some areas of my life and religion.

He explained that the most important truth to understand is this: God is LOVE.

It's a simple concept, really. It is one that I have spoken about many times all over the country. I have written about this in my blog and in other books. And yet, when he laid it out as the basis of the foundation for my Christianity, it felt as though I had never thought of it before. I know that God is love, I have seen evidence of His love, and the more I prostrate myself at His feet every morning and evening, the more I have been begging Him to fill me with His love, so that I may see people as He sees them. God is love—I already knew that—but it wasn't my foundation. It wasn't the essence of the table that would hold up everything else I came to understand about Christ and religion. It was a by-product of my Christianity, but I don't think it was the complete essence of it. Not until now.

"God is love" is the lens through which I should view everything in life. Asscherick said, "A lens is for looking through, not at." So I have been asking myself ever since: How would my theology, my writing, my speaking, my "Christianity" be if the main Truth I wanted others to see is my life-altering and chain-breaking understanding that God is love?

And so I realized that I have some apologies to make . . .

To the girl who lost her virginity at fifteen and was told that her lack of "purity" no longer made her fit for a church pew: I am sorry. We told her that maybe once she got her act together, confessed her sins, went to sexual immorality seminars and could explain to others how it separated her from Christ, maybe then God would want her. I am so sorry. We had it wrong, so painfully wrong. The gift of salvation is not something you can earn, or fix yourself up enough to deserve. When we paint that portrait, we rob Christ of the most beautiful color in His picture: red. God is love. So, regardless of what you have done, regardless of the mistakes you have made, regardless of the sex you traded to feel beautiful, God wants you. We lied to you. God is not a big finger pointing out your mistakes; He is the hand that brushes your hair back while you sob. God is love. I took Him from you.

To the boy who left church in the middle of the message because he was told that God loves everyone *except* homosexuals: I am sorry. Through whispers and feelings of confusion and separation, you believed the lies we fed you that God couldn't want you. As if you needed to overcome your struggles (alone) before you set foot back inside our steeple walls. God has heard your questions, felt your heartache, and doesn't want you staring at Him from the parking lot. I feel especially impressed to remind you that God has never stopped loving you. I robbed you of His everlasting love at that time, and I am so, so sorry. Your brokenness is not too big for God's restorative hands. God has this incredible way of meeting us where we are and yet healing us so that we cannot ever be the same. He still wants you. We were wrong.

To the alcoholic, the pill popper, and the pot smoker: I am sorry. I am sorry I did not understand that sometimes using has a lot less to do with addiction and more to do with a need to dull pain. We looked down our noses at you, we scooted away from you in our seats, and we didn't try at all to hide our distaste with your presence. You were naked and we feared you were contagious. We felt uncomfortable with your idea that

God has room in His heart for you, because it made us feel less special. We want to earn Him, because earning someone's love makes sense to us. But giving love away isn't logical. We have claimed for so long to know Him, and with pride in our hearts we announce to the world that we are His ambassadors. We can quote to you our belief system, we like to teach our understanding of Scripture, and those things are important, but perhaps what we should have done, perhaps the first thing on our agenda, should have been to reflect His true image. God is love. And I am sorry that for so long, I have done a crummy job of revealing that love to you.

To all those I have missed in this apology, please know that He wants you too. I know what it feels like to be told that God loves everyone except you. I know what it feels like to be in the middle of your eighth-grade year and be told by principal and faculty, "You are a bad peach." I know what it feels like to feel the emptiness and nakedness of a world that does not include this pivotal game-changing principle—God is love. I have felt the sting of rejection, and yet somehow, once I had "fixed myself," I forgot.

It reminds me of Martin Luther King Jr.'s statement, "America has given the Negro people a bad check, a check which has come back marked 'insufficient funds.' " The comparison reminds me of the state of many of us in the church. If the church is a bank, all we have in our drawers to hand people is spare change. We have passed love out in bits and pieces to those who have worked hard enough to "deserve it." We have bags filled with gold and silver, and yet all we want to give away is spare change. What if there is not enough treasure for us *and* them? So we give out love in pieces, with strings attached, as if God's love comes with qualifiers. We lied. Compassion is the most defining characteristic of God's character. If we lose our compassion, we lose Christ Himself.

Now I understand why Isaiah cries out, "But we are all like an unclean thing, and all our righteousness is like filthy rags" (Isaiah 64:6, NKJV). On our own, regardless of how great and holy we think we are, we still do not deserve God's love. And yet, in His mercy, He keeps showering us with His love anyway. On a hill called Calvary, He paid the ransom for our sin. You cannot earn God's love. You are naked, and just as you cannot magically clothe yourself, there is no way to make yourself worthy of His love.

None of us deserve it, and yet He keeps giving it to us anyway. And now

I understand that Christ does this, not because He gives love or made love or likes love, but because God *is* love. He is love as much as He is God.

To rob God of His love is like robbing Him of His godliness. It is a part of who He is. I don't know about you, but if there is something on this earth I can do to get these filthy rags a little closer to His righteousness, then count me all in. He saw us naked and ashamed. He watched us trying desperately to cover ourselves to shield our embarrassment. We want to make Him love us, so we try our hardest to work as if this salvation depends on us. Meanwhile, Isaiah 61:10 says, "I delight greatly in the LORD; my soul rejoices in my God. For he has clothed me with garments of salvation and arrayed me in a robe of his righteousness, as a bridegroom adorns his head like a priest, and as a bride adorns herself with her jewels."

When we deserved naked, God provided jewels. When we earned nudity, God clothed us in righteousness. Is it any wonder that on Calvary they crucified Him naked? He took our place, and we took His robe. How dare I not extend that garment to the person next to me? He paid far too great a price for me to delve into spare change.

God is love. That is the truth on which all my other beliefs must rest. That is the lens through which I will see His children and His people. Living life after Eden means we have to paint pictures with His favorite color. We cannot reflect God while handing out spare change. We are brides adorned in jewels so we may share the wealth.

*"Whoever does not love does not know God, because God is love" (1 John 4:8).*

## Share the Naked Truth:

1. Have you ever put restrictions on who God wants?

2. Why is it so hard to love the sinner and hate the sin?

3. In 140 characters, send a message of encouragement to someone who may be struggling spiritually. Tweet/Facebook us *@InLifeAfterEden*.

4. Or Instagram us a photo of your favorite highlighted quote from this reading.

## Day 10 — Seth

# The View From Rock Bottom

Winning provides happiness.
Losing provides wisdom.
—Neil Patel

As we journey together into another valuable lesson in this life after na-ked, I need to share with you a snippet of the restoration process that God has been doing in my life. It touches on the way in which God took me from where I was and slowly started changing me for the better. My hope is that by sharing this with you, you'll be inspired to never stop seeking your Savior, that He may become your most prized and adored possession in this life. I hope that this devotional will revamp your spiritual walk and bring you that much closer to the throne of the One who is able. So let your walk to restoration become a step closer today as you learn the importance of hitting rock bottom.

In 2005 I graduated from high school. I had been feeling the tug of God for some time. He was calling me into ministry. I struggled with the calling because I didn't feel up to par for the job. My mom and stepdad had shipped me off to a little Bible college down south, where I found my-self immersed in chapels and religion classes. I wish I could tell you that everything was downhill from there, but the truth is, I finished that year with almost straight Fs and accumulated the grand total of four college credits. Personal struggles had overcome me, and so I let my college career slip through the cracks. There was no longer a little voice whispering to me that I was a failure, I had a sheet of paper to prove it. F was for failure.

At nineteen years old I had this overwhelming fear that I wouldn't amount to anything. I was conflicted inside over who I was and who God wanted me to be. This intense battle was waging inside my head. I could hear the voice of God beckoning in the midst of my insufficiencies, saying, "Don't give up." And yet at the same time I felt as though I was just one hand's length too far from His grace. Maybe you feel as though you are at a similar crossroad in your life right now. If so, I invite you to keep reading. Rediscover how God's grace is closer than you could ever imagine and how, through failure, life's greatest lessons are often learned.

So there I was, a few days away from finishing out the year. I had neglected all my homework and found myself in a severe state of depression—knowing that I had just flunked yet another round of courses. With no money in my wallet, I couldn't escape to the nearby city and pretend none of this was real. I had hit rock bottom. And this was where I learned that God's grace is never out of reach. Climbing out of my bed, I started pacing the hall of my dorm at 2:30 A.M. I had no peace in my life whatsoever. I knew that things were only going to get worse once my parents caught wind of my grades.

Stressed and mentally exhausted, I peeked through the window of our chapel located on the main floor of the dorm. Hesitating for a minute, I eventually gave the handle a good tug and the door slowly creaked open. Shuffling in, I sat down on an empty pew. It was dead silent, and the only source of light was from the stained-glass portrait of Jesus. I felt as though it had been put there for me and me alone, for this specific moment at this specific time.

What happened next was indescribable. Tears began to fall in buckets, hitting the cold tile beneath my feet. I didn't do anything, I didn't say anything—I didn't feel as though I had to. It was one of the strangest things I have ever experienced in my life. Usually as Christians we come before God and beg for forgiveness over our sins, but this was different. It was as though God was showing me how He really deals with us.

Crying there, I gently rested my head on the pew in front of me, and I felt the hand of God move upon my heart. It didn't condemn me or point out every single sin I had committed those past few months. It simply surrounded me and gave me hope. This is where I learned an important lesson. Christianity isn't about being perfect, nor is it about begging for forgiveness every time you screw up. God is perfect, so you don't have to be. He wants us to ask for forgiveness because in that moment we solidify to ourselves and heaven that God is enough, that He is real. His desire for you is simple: that you come to Him just as you are. That's it. He knows your sin before you confess it, and He knows your brokenness before you call out to Him.

What God wants most of all is you, so give Him the pieces. I wasted so much time running from Him because I was ashamed of what I had done. That year, my failures had wrestled me to the ground time and time again, leaving me pinned by the weight of my own sin. The lesson I learned that day was one that has brought me through many battles since. Hebrews 4:16 says, "Let us then with confidence draw near to the throne of grace, that we may receive mercy and find grace to help in time of need" (ESV). Failure is a given in this life after Eden. My prayer is that you never sit idle, amazed by the enormity of your failure. Instead, find yourself prostrate before a God who is able to bring restoration. I think that is the greater truth.

Don't ever cheapen the sacrifice of Christ by saying your sin is too great, that your failure is too big. Jesus' sacrifice is the common denominator that can make your life whole again. Stop thinking that He can fit into the little box you've created for yourself. Don't ever compare your failures to the person next to you. Everyone needs the grace of God.

I'll never forget one sleepy day of classes. My religion professor, Glenn Russell, stood before us. He paused for a brief second and then slowly started to raise both hands into the air. Lifting one an inch higher than the other, he turned his head to the higher hand and said, "These are the saints." Then he placed his gaze on the hand that was an inch lower and said, "And these are the sinners." He lowered both hands and stared into each person's eyes and closed class with these words: *"It doesn't really matter, does it? It's kind of a level field when it comes to reaching heaven."*

*"Let us then with confidence draw near to the throne of grace,*
*that we may receive mercy and find grace to help in time of*
*need" (Hebrews 4:16, ESV).*

## Share the Naked Truth:

1. What is your biggest spiritual battle right now?

2. In what area of your life do you still need forgiveness from God, and maybe from yourself?

3. In 140 characters, share a verse that will help you pick up your cross and follow Jesus today. Tweet/Facebook us *@InLifeAfterEden.*

4. Or Instagram us a photo of your favorite highlighted quote from this reading.

# I Won't Be Staying Long

You drown, not by falling into a river, but by
staying submerged in it.—Paulo Coelho

First, I see a man and a woman standing outside of a bar. His back is up against the wall, and he rubs his hands down her arms as she shivers. She is already jaded and bent from each time he's exposed her. She's a battered woman, though his fist has never hit her. His morning casualness and tiptoed exits strike her every time. Fully clothed and in eight-inch heels, she stands before him naked. Lacerations on her heart reveal a sad song whose ending she knows. His breath smells like vodka and lies, but she tastes it anyway.

"Let's get you out of the cold," he says, leaning forward and kissing her ear. Her heart is hopeful. He has said all the right things and has kept his attention solely on her, as if she were the most beautiful girl in the room. They've been through this before, but this time will be different. This time he will fall in love with her—she can feel it. Somehow he convinces her that it will be warmer with their clothes off. As I stare at the man, I wonder if he is at all sorry about dressing her with empty words.

"You know I love you," he says, brushing a strand of her hair behind her ear. She hopes he means it this time. But he doesn't. She swigs her whiskey and pouts her lips. She thinks she looks strong, but he watches how her fingers tremble. Each time he kisses her it hurts. She's dreamed for months that he would remember her, and tonight when the cell phone rang, the room stood still, the world stopped spinning, and she clutched her broken heart. She answered and gave him a time and a place and then ran around the room collecting the pieces of her dignity and trying to press them into form. She bats the lashes of her eyes, and she imagines him being entranced by their rhythm. He's not, but he pretends well.

As he lays her down, he glances out the window to make sure his truck engine is running. He won't be staying long.

\* \* \* \* \*

In another image I see a woman. Her phone finally rang with the name she had been praying would call. Her fingers stiffened as she fumbled to press the correct button that would close the gap on their distance. His voice would sound like music, and she couldn't wait for her favorite song.

"Are you OK?" she asked while biting her lip. She squeezed her eyes shut tight and held her breath.

"I'm still OK," he whispered, but his voice cracked.

They talked about all he had seen. The death he had met. He told her that the ground reeked of sweat and blood and how he hated that he was growing used to the smell. His lips were dry, and he licked them again. He told her about the children screaming. They had told him there would be shrieks, but no one told him about the children. He swallowed tears, and his eyes ached from suppressing them for nine months. She told her soldier how she wasn't sleeping well, and that felt familiar to him, because neither had he. Every time he closed his eyes he saw himself placing a black cloth bag over the head of a man he didn't know. He had never had so many dreams about one stranger. He felt connected to him now, in a strange way more than all the other men he'd ever known. No one had said what happened to the stranger, and he knew better than to ask.

"I don't think I can ever do that again," he said aloud. In the distance he heard the screaming children, though he hadn't seen them in hours. Their cries were background noise in his mind, like a song stuck on repeat. "You'll get used to it," his friend had said. The vacant stare on his face told him that this is what he was afraid of.

"I miss you," she whispered.

He swallowed the lump in his throat and tried shushing the screaming children. He wanted to be in the present moment with her, but the past was too vicious.

"Shut up," he barked out loud, trying to quiet the faded tears of the children jammed in the closets of his mind. "I am trying to talk to my wife!"

"What?" she asked, confused by his delirium.

He was afraid to open up those closet doors. There was no one around who could help him close them. "I'm sorry," he answered her. "I won't be staying long."

* * * * *

In the next picture I see a little boy. He creeps up the stairs to his mother's room. The door has just slammed, and the yelling has stopped. He hopes his father has left for the night. He hears her stifled tears the closer he gets to the edge of her bed. It's the sound of pain and sadness strangled by a pillowcase. He couldn't miss that sound anywhere. It's the sound of his childhood.

He pushes the door open, and she lifts her eyes to meet his. Her eyes are swollen, and one is bruised. Purple fingerprints are left around the most beautiful neck he has ever seen. She is an angel, and feathers are lying all over the bedroom floor. He wants to pick them up, to gather them together and make them whole again. He wants to glue her halo together, but it has been smashed to smithereens. The glow of her angelic figure is growing dimmer by the second. She is clothed, and yet she is naked, and so he averts his eyes to give her privacy.

"You need to leave him," he says, hoisting his body up next to hers and throwing his arms around her waist. She squeezes him tightly and sniffs his hair. It smells like innocence. She inhales deeper.

"It's not that simple." She begins again her sordid lines of excuses. They'd have no money, no resources, no home. Where would they go?

"Anywhere," he whispers, and tears start to run. She inhales again, but something's different. His hair smells less innocent. Her throat closes, and her eyes bulge.

"I couldn't live if he killed you," says the nine-year-old boy whose eyes

79

look ninety. Suddenly he sees it, a resolve in her eyes he hasn't seen before. Something has struck her, something has changed. Seizing the moment, he continues on. He pats her hair with one hand, and with the other he collects her feathers. She will need them if she is going to fly, he thinks.

"I promise you," she says with a glare of determination he knows is genuine, "we won't be staying long."

\* \* \* \* \*

In the next image I see a school. The hallways are filled with teenagers and classrooms run by teachers. Cool kids and not-so-cool kids sit in a cafeteria that is as segregated as 1967. He had gone to the principal's office once. He tried to tell him that the teasing was going to make him snap and that the spitballs were driving him crazy. The abuse at school was slightly less toxic than the abuse at home, but either way the poison was making him grow sicker.

"Tough it out," he was told. He learned from his video games that tough men strapped guns to their sides, and if they didn't like people, they killed them. He'd become a man himself. Life was a script, and he'd rewrite how his ended. They would see how tough he was. Instead of cologne, he covers himself in gunpowder, and instead of books he fills his backpack with metal. This will be just like his favorite game, only this time he is done playing.

He cast a glance back at his mirror, and what he saw confused him. He was naked. He had never been so disrobed. He touched the mirror to see what was happening, and suddenly the mirage was gone. He left his home and stepped into his high school, completely oblivious that the nakedness had swallowed him. The quiet voice in his head that told him that they deserved it grew louder, and he got colder.

There is a beautiful girl with long brown hair, blood seeping out from her abdomen. A fifteen-year-old kid with a vendetta and a gun is hell-bent on making them all pay. She had laughed when he asked her to prom. How dare she? It was a question, not a joke, and now she'd know the difference.

"Isn't funny now, is it?" he asks, standing over her dead body. He turns, and his face is twisted. He looks familiar to the other kids in the hallway, but just barely. His eyes are narrower, and his skin is paler. His jaw tightens, and the shadow he casts screams pure evil. He pulls the trigger three more times, this time just firing at random moving targets. A boy in a corner struggles for air but can't find any. Cops yell, "Drop the gun!" and the fifteen-year-old with his hand on the trigger presses it to his skull.

"No need," he says calmly. "Because I won't be staying long."

\* \* \* \* \*

Last, I see a cemetery. I run my fingers along the headstones and brush dirt from the names. Thousands upon thousands of dreams rest here, and the thought of it suffocates me. I see the beds of lovers sleeping side by side, and babies swallowed by their graves. Tears spill from my eyes, and the sun burns my skin. "This world looks a lot like this cemetery," I moan to myself.

Just then, the heavens part and a trumpet blares. I shade my eyes from a brilliant light and hear the chorus of angels sing. Each angel holds a robe of light, and the beauty of its brilliance blinds me.

"Don't worry," the Lord's voice echoes like thunder rolling, "I am coming to bring My faithful to Me." I see the finger of a man pointing at every grave I just cried over.

"They won't be staying long."

> *"For the Lord himself will come down from heaven, with a loud command, with the voice of the archangel and with the trumpet call of God, and the dead in Christ will rise first"*
> *(1 Thessalonians 4:16).*

**Share the Naked Truth:**

1. What is something you can do today to help someone who may be struggling?

2. Why do you think the world is so violent today?

3. In 140 characters, give the URL to one news headline from this week that reminds you this world is ending. Tweet/Facebook us *@InLifeAfterEden.*

4. Or Instagram us a photo of your favorite highlighted quote from this reading.

## Day 12 — Seth

# Life Is but a Moment

Life is a succession of moments. To live each one
is to succeed.—Corita Kent

If someone were to take a snapshot of your life, what would they see? Would the moments they capture be filled with time you spent at the office, working for that big house, or drooling over owning that fancy car? I am not condemning nice things, but if the snapshots of our lives are filled with more job moments, house moments, self-moments, then you and I have forgotten the purpose of this life.

I recently gave a talk on Christian education at my ten-year high school reunion. Focusing my eyes beyond the glare of the stage lights, I looked at the well-manicured audience in front of me. Some people looked exactly the same as the last time I saw them ten years earlier. Some seemed to have found their place in the world. Nice clothes and confident smiles lit up the room. As the special music came to a close, the perfectly executed notes lingered in my ears, soothing my nerves. It was then that it hit me. What is the true purpose to this occasion, after all? Was it to show up in our BMWs or flashy suits and ties?

It was in that moment, just before I stood up to speak, that God was convicting me. I wasn't there to give a nice speech about the importance of Christian education. I was there because God wanted to speak to me, first and foremost. Somehow I had fallen onto the slippery slope of living the American dream. The past few weeks, all my energies had been spent on dreaming about a property that had just become available down the street from us. It wasn't just any property, it was my dream property—a house on a lake. I had instantly thrown our house on the market to follow this dream of mine. I barely consulted my family, I barely consulted my wife, and I barely consulted God. I wanted that house, and I was determined to force everyone into seeing why this was a must-have home.

Despite it being out of my family's budget, I went for it. I overstepped my means, and I thought of 101 reasons to justify my decision. It wasn't until I sat on that stage to give a speech on the value of Christian education that everything hit me. How could I have moved so quickly on that house? I had talked things over with people—to convince them, not to listen to their advice. I also had given little attention to the kind of financial predicament this could cause for my family down the road. All I saw was the opportunity to live the American dream—and I wanted it.

God convicted me that evening that this wasn't His plan for me. I wondered later that night, on the hour drive home, how many people in that audience had taken their knowledge of Christ and pushed it aside for a moment of earthly gain? I am not condemning nice houses or cars, but if we kill ourselves financially to keep up with the Kardashians, well, then maybe we should reconsider what drives us to get up each morning.

Are we driven by the fear that if we fall one paycheck behind we'll have a late payment on our mortgage because we are living beyond our means? Or is our reason for living to give the glory to God? I had what I call a God-moment that evening. Maybe you're having one right now? At the core of our existence, the reason for breathing must be this innate longing to have God-moments. And these can only happen if we find ourselves synced with His will.

If we spend more time stressing over our fancy houses, pristine lawns, and that shiny Beemer in our driveway, we've missed the point. Those moments are worthless. Sorry. When God bursts through the clouds with mighty thunder, robed in blinding majesty, I am highly skeptical that He will look at my lawn, car, or house and say, *"Well done, My good and faithful servant."* I don't know about you, but I want that moment when Christ returns to be a moment that falls into perfect bliss because of the way I've used my time here on earth prior to His coming. Nice things are fine, but if our pride in life starts and stops with perfection here on earth, then we've missed the boat.

I want a life filled with moments of helping others. I want a life that is dedicated to God and family. Somehow we've taken our high school diplomas and college degrees and invested them in a life that is centered on self. We work harder because the world screams in our ear, "You must have this car, live in this house, and wear these clothes!" So we kill ourselves in order to live the American dream, while our kids never see us, and our marriage crumbles. We are so busy rushing to the fancy office to make money 365 days a year that we've passed by that soup kitchen 365 days a year, on our way to "success." We are far too busy for volunteer work. Success is hard work.

How in the world can Christ return, let alone say, "Well done!" if this is all that our Christianity has amounted to? Perhaps we have taken our diplomas, our Christ-centered focus, and turned it into something else. By the end of the week we are so exhausted from our jobs and stress in life that we have forgotten the very essence of what this life is all about. Moments, precious moments, that you and I will never get back. Maybe we are so busy looking for perfect, we forgot the power that actually enables us to live perfect.

Families suffer, marriages crumble, and addictions set in, all in the name of living the American dream. If we truly opened our eyes, maybe we would see that our big success is really nothing more than big emptiness. It's a big void, filled with big houses, when it should be filled with big families and big desires for God. What have you done with the moments that God has given you today? Can I suggest that you call your widowed grandma that you haven't talked to in quite a while, or lend a hand to someone in need? You'd be surprised at all the good that can come from replacing one text with one phone call. It would only take a moment.

Perhaps you've been financially blessed, and yet you can't remember the last time you have relieved someone else's financial burden. Take one moment and look up. That's a moment worth waiting for, isn't it? The greatest God-moment this earth has ever seen is just a few moments around the corner.

Revelation chapters 1–3 speak about the seven churches. We believe that the final church—the church of Laodicea—is where we are in earth's history. And Laodicea is the final church before Christ returns. It is also described as being lukewarm—neither hot nor cold. It's a church that is complacent, a materialistic church. With that said, here is perhaps the most noticeable distinguishing characteristic of all: with the previous six churches, the church waits on God to move, but in the final hour of earth's history, it is God who is waiting on the church: "Behold, I stand at the door and knock. If anyone hears My voice and opens the door, I will come in to him and dine with him, and he with Me" (Revelation 3:20, NKJV).

Laodicea, God is calling us today. Let's open the door and let Him in. Scripture gives us the key that opens the door. It's found in the gospel of Matthew: "And he who does not take his cross and follow after Me is not worthy of Me. He who has found his life will lose it, and he who has lost his life for My sake will find it" (Matthew 10:38, 39, NKJV). Where we'll spend the moments of eternity is determined by how we spend the moments we've each individually been given daily. It is a universal question that demands an individual response.

A few years ago I made the trek back to school full time. My wife and I took a huge leap of faith because she didn't have full-time employment yet. She was an adjunct teacher at her community college. We would be giving up our good health insurance and financial security. I have to tell you that we faced some pretty tough times. I can remember my children tugging at my ankles and saying, "Daddy, we're hungry." I was always able to put something into their mouths—even if it was just a bowl of cereal or a pancake.

Did you know that today there are still 153 million orphan boys and girls who would do anything in this world to have someone give them just one bowl of cereal or a pancake? As you tuck yourself in under your warm blankets this evening, think long and hard about what you're living for. When you know the answer to that, you know the value you have personally placed on the moments you've been given.

*"Keep your life free from love of money, and be content with what you have, for he has said, 'I will never leave you nor forsake you'" (Hebrews 13:5, ESV).*

**Share the Naked Truth:**

1. What do the moments of your life consist of?

2. Do you think any part of you has bought into the American dream? Why or why not?

3. In 140 characters, write about a service moment you can commit to doing before you finish reading this book. Tweet/Facebook us *@InLifeAfterEden.*

4. Or Instagram us a photo of your favorite highlighted quote from this reading.

## Day 13 — Heather

# Set Your Alarm

Lose an hour in the morning and you will be all
day hunting for it.—Richard Whately

I have recently been praying circles around one request: that Christ
would allow me to experience a personal relationship with Him. This is
life after Eden. If I want to feel less bare, I need more of Him and less of
me. I have asked if He will allow me to know Him and experience Him
as intimately as I know and experience my own husband. I don't want to
love Him as this distant God of ancient days; I want to love Him as my
personal God. When people ask me about God's character, I want to be
able to describe who He is, not just because Scripture tells me these are
His attributes but because my life has seen those attributes fulfilled. This
has been my prayer, and it is part of how I have been trying to survive life
after Eden. I want to tell you one of the ways I have already seen Him
answering it.

I want to share this with you because I know I am not alone. I know
there are others out there just like me, praying this same prayer. I know
there are others who don't want to love Him the way a child loves a father
who works all day, whom they never get to see or play with, or have intimate one-on-one time with. I know we don't just want to love Him for
the authority of His position but because of the power He has displayed
through our relationship. I want a personal God like the one Adam and
Eve had in Eden.

I have seen Him answering this prayer in my life, and so I had to write it down and share with you how I am coming to know Him and love Him not just as a father but as a daddy.

Are you ready? Here is the secret sauce to my current prayer life and what I think will help you live in life after Eden: I set my alarm.

It sounds simple, but let me draw the lines. Clearly, I think the first thing we have to do is seek Him. First we have to actually pray these intentional prayers like the ones I described above. God says He will grant our requests, but He also says we must come and ask Him. First, we must ask Him for a more personal relationship, but then we have to set our alarm. This is what I have been doing in my own spiritual life. I had been doing it for a few weeks and felt convicted of it when I discovered I wasn't the only one drawing this conclusion. I was affirmed in my philosophy when I read this quote from best-selling author Mark Batterson the other day: "I'm more and more convinced that the biggest difference between success and failure, both spiritually and occupationally, is your waking-up time on your alarm clock."[*]

Before reading this in Batterson's book, I felt God telling me that the time I was spending with Him was not enough. Mind you, I had committed nearly a year earlier to spending time with Him intentionally, reading Scripture and in prayer three times a day, as the prophet Daniel has modeled. You can imagine my slight discomfort when I felt that He had told me, "It is still not enough . . . if you want to have a personal relationship with Me of the caliber and intimacy you are requesting, this is simply not enough."

I took a few days to swallow that down, and then I asked my next question. "OK, so what do I do different?" I felt Him telling me that I needed to be setting my alarm. He wanted me to get up an hour earlier, read my Scripture, and then discuss my life with Him in prayer. That was it.

It seems perhaps like an easy task, but for me it was again hard to swallow. I value my sleep. As I write this, I have two small children under the age of two, I am in the beginning stages of an intensive dissertation process for my PhD, and I teach five classes at the collegiate level. I am often just . . . well . . . tired. I did not want to get up an hour earlier than I was already getting up, but I felt God saying that if I wanted to really

---

[*] Mark Batterson, *The Circle Maker* (Grand Rapids, MI: Zondervan, 2011), 142.

know Him, this was the sacrifice He wanted from me.

In Old Testament times the Israelites were required to make constant sacrifices. It was how they were to acknowledge a real God and not a distant one. They erected altars, sacrificed their flocks, and gave something they valued back to God in order to signify that He was above all of it. What do you give back to God in order to signify that He is the supreme leader in your life? A lot of times we Christians discuss our religion in terms of what we do not do, but it is good to spend more time thinking about what you *do* that symbolizes your faith.

Doing physical things for God often changes the relationship. I used to say my prayers sitting up, but about five years ago I realized how different my prayers were when I got down on my knees and placed my head to the floor. My physical position affected my spiritual one. That is the only position I pray in now, for the most part. Sometimes I am tired, I am already in bed, and I realize I need to pray. The last thing I want to do is get out of my warm bed, get on my knees, and press my face to the floor. I do it anyway. I do it because it reminds me that I am dust and He is God, and our relationship should never be based on what makes me comfortable but what keeps me reminded that He is God.

You should try it. I know it sounds as though it wouldn't matter, but it does. I did not even think of it as unique anymore until a friend traveled with me to a speaking engagement. In the hotel room I asked them to pray with me, and then I immediately dropped to the floor and pressed my face to it. For a moment there was an awkward silence, and I wondered why. And then I realized that I looked pretty extreme. The truth is, though, that if God were actually in your presence, you wouldn't be standing. It would not be enough for you to be on your knees with your head bowed. You wouldn't sit still and just close your eyes to show reverence. The presence of His holiness would cause you to fall forward. Your mouth would be in the dirt, and you would not dare raise your gaze. I want to pray to God as though He is actually in my presence, and that small physical act has humbled me toward Him.

Now there was another physical sacrifice I felt God was calling me to make. I needed to set my alarm. He wanted me to get up earlier. It was one extra hour. So little when you think about the depth of my request. I wanted to intimately know the Creator of the universe, and He was happy to do it, if I would get up one hour earlier each morning. In retrospect I am saddened that I was so torn over His request. I should have been thrilled that my Redeemer would even say, "Yes, I will show Myself to you. You may know Me intimately." I should have been elated about the blessing this would be and how it would multiply blessings in my life, and yet strangely somehow my human nature had me looking at this extra hour as a cost.

This is part of life after Eden. I live in sin, and my heart is naturally inclined to do the wrong things. To be honest, I am still learning how to pay tithe and not feel as if I am losing something. I know God is merciful, because I am the most unholy person and yet He keeps using me anyway. People see me up front to speak, and they think that somehow, because I am writing books and speaking regularly, that I have it all figured out, that I have conquered sin and can wear a crown. The truth is that I am just as naked today as I was ten years ago. The only difference is that I recognize it now, and I am constantly pestering God to bring me closer to Him. He has been, and I assure you it is not because of my holiness, but rather my persistence in wanting to change. I think that is truly all God wants from us. He wants us to want Him and to pursue Him.

Let's face it, the disciples were hardly stellar converts. They fought, swore, lied, and practiced violence. Surely God could have found twelve holier men, and yet these twelve hooligans would develop the Christian church and change the world forever. What was their secret? Why did God not give up on them and throw in the towel after the first time they completely missed the boat? Well, they wanted Him. They pursued Him, they left their homes for Him. They went to sleep at His feet and woke up beside them. They were hardly holy, but they knew that He was, and so they grabbed on like a chokehold. I truly think that is all God wants from us. He doesn't expect us to fix ourselves. He wants us to want Him and let Him do the fixing. He wants us to constantly place ourselves at His feet. He wants us to recognize our need for Him. He will do the rest.

I should note here that, as of yet, I have never heard the voice of God audibly. It is a prayer I pray on a regular basis, that He would let me hear His voice, but so far, we just aren't there. I tell Him frequently that I don't need some huge message of prophecy. I will be content just to hear His voice tell me He loves me. Just once. That's it, and I can die happy. I have met a few people in my lifetime who say that they have heard Him audibly. Their character forces me to believe them. Sometimes I wonder why them and not me. I want that intimacy with Him. Either He doesn't want to talk about it, or silence is part of His answer.

I have been much more in tune with His still, small whisper guiding my thoughts in the past year. I have heard Him in my mind tell me to do or not do something—to talk to someone, to give to someone, to start something, to write it down. I have heard Him in my mind directing me on these things, and I am beyond convinced that it was Him, based on the fruit it has born. I am grateful for that.

Once I heard Him tell me to give the cash in my wallet to one of my students. I told Him no. That was weird. It was inappropriate. I only had twenty dollars, and I didn't even know her. I had students who stayed after class and chatted with me. She was not one of them. "Give her the money, Heather," I heard several times, and each time I protested. At the end of class they all rushed out. It was the last day before spring break. "How can I trust you with big things when you are still unfaithful on small things?" I heard Him say in my mind.

"Fine, God!" I told him. "I'll find her." I ran like a mad woman through the parking lot. I couldn't find her.

That spring break I went to Mexico. I had a wonderful week standing as the maid of honor in my best friend's wedding. I didn't think of the girl or the twenty dollars even once. When I got back to school, her class came in. As they went for their seats, I saw her, and again in my head I heard, "Give her the cash in your wallet." This time it was forty dollars—God had doubled it.

At the end of class I asked her to stay back. She obliged, afraid she was in trouble.

"Look," I said, "I know this is weird and doesn't make any sense, but I feel like I am supposed to give you this money. I don't know why, and I have never done this with a student, and if I have offended you, I am sorry."

She looked at me shell-shocked. Suddenly this tough girl burst into tears. "Right before I walked into class," she said, "I was talking to my friend. I am a single mom at eighteen years old. I grew up in foster care, so I don't have parents to help me. I asked my friend if she had any money at lunch because I had to buy diapers after this class. She said no, but we could call her dad. I called and I asked him if he had any money for diapers. He said he was sorry but he didn't have any extra money this week. I cried with her, and she said we should pray. I haven't prayed in a long time, but I did right before this class, and I said 'God, can You just help me get enough money for diapers?' I didn't know how He could or if He would, but I prayed. And now, after class, you are handing me forty dollars, a little bit more than it will cost me to purchase a large box of diapers."

She sobbed, and then I sobbed. We hugged, and I grabbed her shoulders and looked her in the eyes. "I promise you this money is not coming from me. In fact, God asked me to give it to you before spring break, and I didn't want to. I am doing it today because He has told me to. This money is not from me, it is from God, and He is just using me in this instance." To this day, I still take care of that student with my extra money each month. She goes to school full time, works full-time hours at McDonalds, and is the strongest woman I know. Sometimes she will call me and say she can't do it. She doesn't have the time or energy to keep living this way. I tell her that she can and she will finish school for her daughter. Her daughter is gorgeous and full of life, and she will not remember the struggle they experienced these first few years. All she will know is that her mother worked hard to become a teacher and that she admires her with all her heart. I don't know if I could have heard God so clearly, had I not been setting my alarm for our worship time each morning.

And so I still set my alarm. I pray that if I give up the extra hour of sleep, He will sustain me and I wouldn't feel too excruciatingly tired. He has. What has resulted in these early morning hours is a fruitful relationship with Him that I promise you I had never known before. I want to stress that I loved Him before this. I have loved God my whole life. And yet our journey together has really hit a turning point in the last couple of years. I want more, though. And so I set my alarm.

I have since realized that going to work with a short Scripture read and short prayer, or sometimes (if I was running late) barely anything at all,

signaled to myself subconsciously that I can make myself successful. If I
dared ever set foot outside my house without first worshiping at the feet of
the King whose very word sustains my life, I was shortchanging myself. I
was shortchanging my students, my peers, my children, and my husband.
I thought that I could be an effective teacher, mother, wife, and peer without Him. I thought that I could wake up on my own and still expect God
to make me a blessing to those around me. How could I bless them without clinging to Him first? I had clearly missed the point. And since I have
rectified this, I have a better understanding of why the prophet Daniel
prayed three times a day. There is nothing good in us without Him. I had
subconsciously set myself up to believe that I was strong enough to face
this world without consciously asking Him to go before me. I was wrong.

Now, after setting my alarm, and spending that hour in the morning
reading His Word and getting on my knees before Him in prayer, I am
consciously reminding myself that I need Him. I need Him before anything has even happened yet—before the stress of my dissertation, before
the screaming and fighting of children, before the question from a student
that I don't have the answer to. I acknowledge that I am a broken vessel
who needs Him to surround me with His grace.

Last, you should know that blessings have already started to rain. I have
had doors open already that I could never have even dreamed of. Greater
than these earthly blessings of financial or professional development that
I am experiencing is this new level of intimacy with my Lord that I have
found. He is a really awesome God, and I am discovering it for myself.

I dare say, openly and publicly, that I, Heather Thompson Day, am de-
veloping a personal and intimate relationship with Jesus, the One whom
they called Christ. In the early hours of the morning, when I cry to Him,
He has revealed Himself to me in ways that I had never before experienced. I cannot believe that I almost missed this by not setting my alarm.

I will leave you with the words of Mark Batterson, who proved to me that
this is not just an isolated phenomenon with God that only I am meant to
experience. It is a promise that He would keep for you also—just ask Him:

"I'm more and more convinced that the biggest difference between success and failure, both spiritually and occupationally, is your waking-up
time on your alarm clock."

# Set Your Alarm

*"Awake, my glory! Awake, harp and lyre! I will awaken
the dawn. I will give thanks to You, O Lord, among the
peoples; I will sing praises to You among the nations"
(Psalm 57:8, 9, NKJV).*

## Share the Naked Truth:

1. Would you be willing to set your alarm earlier for the next week in
   order to have worship?

2. How much time do you typically spend reading the Bible each day?

3. In 140 characters, write a commitment of how much time you will
   spend alone in Scripture this week, and what time you will set your
   alarm to do that. Tweet/Facebook us *@InLifeAfterEden.*

4. Or Instagram us a photo of your favorite highlighted quote from this
   reading.

# And It Begins Again . . .

Procrastination is one of the most common
and deadliest of diseases and its toll on
success and happiness is heavy.
—Wayne Gretzky

One of the most interesting stories from the American Revolution involved Colonel Johann Rall and his Hessian troops, who were stationed in Trenton, New Jersey. All was calm one evening as the men rallied around a leisurely game of cards. The air was still, and all that could be heard was the chirping of crickets in the nearby thicket. With all defenses down, Colonel Rall and his men became engrossed in a game of cards. Shuffling the cards through his fingers like a pro, Rall dealt one hand after another.

One of Rall's men placed an envelope next to the deck of cards in front of him. Shifting his focus for a split-second, Rall decided that it was no emergency and quickly pressed the letter into his front pants pocket, saying to himself, "I'll open it when the game is finished." He did not know that inside the sealed envelope were a few very important words—vital information that General George Washington was just beyond the horizon. Soon, Washington and his men were just moments away from Rall's post in Trenton.

When Colonel Rall finally opened the crinkled envelope, panic quickly sucked the oxygen out of the room. Gasping for breath, he and his men tried to rush into formation, but it was too late. You see, those few precious moments made the difference between life and death for Rall and his men that day. If only he had placed more significance and urgency on that crinkled envelope instead of slipping it into his pocket, history would have turned out much different.

I am certain that many Christians today have somehow fallen into the same dilemma as the colonel. We sit in full uniform, giving off the appearance that we're ready for battle, yet at the same time we are living life as though we're playing a casual game of cards on a peaceful evening. The problem with this mode of thinking is that for many of us, life ends before the game does.

What if we placed more importance on the letter that each of us has been given? It is our letter that has been perfectly pressed and presented to us in the form of a story—the gospel. How many of us have even taken the time to read it, cover to cover? Isn't it strange that we will spend so much time telling other people about a God that we ourselves haven't even taken the time to fully read about? The Bible contains words of wisdom and guidance for the battle we're in. It is the lens through which we are to scrutinize every action. It is our key for surviving the battle and, ultimately, the war, in victory.

If we could only see tomorrow, maybe we would see that tomorrow isn't coming. I am not talking scare tactics here, but if we forget that we're in the front lines of battle, then we'll forget the reason why we have the Bible altogether. It's our envelope, and it's sealed with the blood of Christ.

The Barna Group did a study in 2013 and found that nearly 61 percent of evangelical Christians say they have read the Bible through.* The largest demographic of those numbers is, of course, baby boomers. Conversely, Lifeway Research did a study and found that only 19 percent of Christians who claim to have the "desire to please God and honor Him in all they do" actually read the Bible daily.† Only 19 percent!

Daily Bible reading is not just about seeking purity, but it is also about acknowledging that we cannot live purely without constant saturation in His Word. Avid Bible reading tells God we are aware that we cannot do

---

* Barna Group, "The Books American Are Reading," research release, June 13, 2013, https://www.barna.org/barna-update/culture/614-the-books-americans-are-reading.

† Jeremy Weber, "80% of Churchgoers Don't Read Bible Daily, LifeWay Survey Suggests," *Christianity Today*, September 7, 2012, http://www.christianitytoday.com/gleanings/2012/september/80-of-churchgoers-dont-read-bible-daily-lifeway-survey.html.

this without Him. In this life after Eden, nothing is more important to realize than that the enemy is just around the corner, and we need to spend time in God's Word.

Scripture screams this message through every word that is penned in the story. This is the message Christ spoke as He seeks to draw our attention back to the story of Noah in the book of Genesis. It is the inward belief that every minute is crucial; it reflects the direct, outward action of humanity. One of the devil's greatest devices is to lure us into a state of procrastination and leisure by getting us caught up in a little bit of pleasure and fun, thinking preparation for the fight can wait.

In Matthew 24:37–39 we find this warning given by Jesus concerning procrastination: "But of that day and hour no one knows, not even the angels of heaven, but My Father only. But as the days of Noah were, so also will the coming of the Son of Man be. For as in the days before the flood, they were eating and drinking, marrying and giving in marriage, until the day that Noah entered the ark, and did not know until the flood came and took them all away, so also will the coming of the Son of Man be" (NKJV).

It was life as usual for Colonel Rall. He read the letter only when he had finished his card game. It is hard to look at Colonel Rall's story and miss its significance for ours. Jesus says, "And they were drinking, marrying and giving in marriage, until the day that Noah entered the ark."

In order to understand the full theological impact of Christ's words in the gospel of Matthew 24, we need to go back to the story of Noah in Genesis 6 and grasp what it meant in Noah's time. Verse 2 reads, "The sons of God saw the daughters of men," indicating there are two groups of people. Gill's *Exposition of the Entire Bible* makes a logical assessment about who the "sons of God" are: God's chosen. He states, " . . . but rather this is to be understood of the posterity of Seth, who from the times of Enosh, when then began to be called by the name of the Lord, (Genesis 4:25) had the title of the sons of God."*

So if these are God's people, then who are the "daughters of men"? Genesis 4:15 says, "And the Lord set a mark on Cain, lest anyone finding him should kill him." This is very important. Take note that God said this

---

* John Gill's *Exposition of the Entire Bible*, commentary on Genesis 6:2.

concerning Cain's act of killing his brother Abel. This brings clarity to who these two groups of people are. God's people are the "sons of God"—the pure bloodline of Adam—who became defiled by intermarrying with the impure "daughters of men" or the descendants of Cain. This makes logical sense in light of the fact that Genesis 4 has just delineated for us the line of Cain, or the sons and daughters of men, and Genesis 5 delineates the sons of Seth, or sons and daughters of God.

Note also that Genesis 6:2 says they defiled themselves because the daughters of men were "beautiful" and they "took wives for themselves of all whom they chose." This reminds us of the fact that sin often appears attractive and desirable but in the end leads to death. Perhaps this is why Jesus said these words concerning Noah's time in Matthew 24: "But as the days of Noah were, so also will the coming of the Son of Man be" (verse 37, NKJV).

*The Telegraph*, a British newspaper, reported the results of study in the *Journal of Experimental and Social Psychology* that showed how men are affected by speaking to an attractive woman. "The research shows men who spend even a few minutes in the company of an attractive woman perform less well in tests designed to measure brain function than those who chat to someone they do not find attractive. Researchers who carried out the study, published in the Journal of Experimental and Social Psychology, think the reason may be that men use up so much of their brain function or 'cognitive resources' trying to impress beautiful women, they have little left for other tasks."*

Perhaps, in the book of Genesis, God's people had a poor cognitive response to obeying God's instructions, simply because they lingered too long in the midst of temptation. I think Eve would concur. Maybe temptation caused them to procrastinate in the mission that God had originally called them to. The lives that they were originally designed to live were to bring glory to God, and instead they slowly put the focus on the pleasures that gratified self.

I believe as young men and women we will surely fall into sin if we allow

---

* Pat Hagan, "Men Lose Their Minds Speaking to Pretty Women," *The Telegraph*, September 3, 2009, http://www.telegraph.co.uk/news/health/news/6132718/Men-lose-their-minds-speaking-to-pretty-women.html.

our eyes to feast on the *beauty* of this world. Do you hear me? I think Joseph knew his victory over the seductress wife of Potiphar came only from turning the other way and running. Some close friends of mine are going through a sticky time right now. They are only two years into their marriage, and things don't look good. Why? Because what started as an innocent, flirtatious gesture to another person has now manifested itself in a full-blown affair. Run, don't walk away from temptation. Joseph nailed it.

And so the sons of God abandoned the beauty of God's word and followed after the desires of their hearts, indulging in the pleasures around them. They traded the glorious splendor of God's promise to prosper them, protect them, and preserve them for a slow fade into darkness and sin. The people were given a time prophecy in Genesis 6:3. It was 120 years—a sufficient time to repent.

Notice the expression in Genesis 6:3, "for he is indeed flesh." It comes from the Hebrew word *shagag*, meaning "to wander" or "go astray." *The Seventh-day Adventist Bible Commentary* tells us that God's people in Genesis 6 had denied the Holy Spirit to the point of complete deafness to His calling. Today God is calling a generation of young men and women who have surrendered themselves to the will of God.

God could have wiped everyone out, even Noah, and completely started over. Had He done this, though, the devil would have won in his accusations about God. It is easy to wipe out people; it is much harder to wipe out words that have already been spun. In the story of Genesis we learn how the preservation of Noah and his family proves that God would have come to this earth to die the death of a criminal for only eight, and I dare say, for only one person. Don't ever say that your life doesn't hold unmeasurable meaning in the eyes of God. And don't ever say that someone else's life doesn't matter.

Colonel Rall rejected that letter of warning and grace when it was handed to him by his courier, only opening it when it was too late. Our letter of warning and grace is found in the pages of Scripture. We should open it now.

Now I know what you're thinking—probably the same thing as me. I read my Bible, I know my Scripture, I know the signs of the times. But do we?

During the 1800s when our church was being formed, J. N. Andrews and others gathered around candlelight to read Scripture habitually. When someone asked Andrews the question in probably a joking manner, "J. N., could you reproduce the Bible if we lost it?" he responded, "No, but I could produce almost the entire New Testament."

That's humbling for those of us who think we have what it takes. We think we are righteous because of our knowledge. But I am telling you, there is a vast difference between being righteous and being self-righteous. God is calling us back to a deeper study and understanding of His Word. We should be focused as never before. That is how a generation of old and young can claim the name "sons of God." If you are suited up in your battle gear but sitting around playing cards, you are doing it wrong.

*"As the days of Noah were, so also will the coming of the*
*Son of Man be" (Matthew 24:37, NKJV).*

### Share the Naked Truth:

1. Are there any temptations you may have allowed yourself to linger around?

2. If you had to give a rough estimate of when God will return, what would you say and why? Ten years? Twenty? Thirty?

3. In 140 characters, write what you think the letter would say if a courier from heaven showed up at your doorstep. Tweet/Facebook us *@InLifeAfterEden*.

4. Or Instagram us a photo of your favorite highlighted quote from this reading.

## Day 15 — Heather

# The Church Reformers

Lord Jesus, it is for thee that I patiently endure
this cruel death. I pray thee to have mercy
on my enemies.—John Huss

John Huss is considered to be one of the first church reformers. Not only did Huss have to navigate a world in life after Eden, but he made the ultimate sacrifice. John Huss was burned at the stake for heresy. We are told that when Huss was arrested and informed that he would be torched for his faith, he purposely practiced holding his hand over fire to prepare for his final test. He burned himself in preparation. He wanted to be faithful to the end. He wanted to be completely and utterly prepared.

I believe we are nearing the last-day ministry that began at the Reformation of Luther and John Huss. It is why Seth and I work with my father at Final Cry Ministries. The signs are everywhere, and each day I am more burdened that this world is about to undergo a dramatic controversy of epic proportions.

But here is a thought I have been having: What if God is not waiting for the world to grow darker but rather for the church to grow brighter? What if the return of Heaven and a chorus of angels all hinge on a generation rising up with a distinct commitment to faithfulness? Is it possible that the return of Christ is dependent on a return to Eden? What if God doesn't want us naked but would prefer that we adorned our bodies with salvation? What if all of heaven was waiting on a smoke signal from . . . well . . . you?

# The Church Reformers

Men and women gave their lives rather than bend what they believed to be unmovable biblical truth during the Reformation. They were imprisoned, publicly flogged, tortured, and some, like Huss, were burned at the stake. The strange thing is that for many Reformers, like Huss, the death they met was by choice. Many begged Luther to recant; he could have met the same fate as Huss. Surely he had an image in his mind of the burnt flesh on Huss's hands. But rather than go back on his convictions, he chose to move forward in truth.

I have been to Rome. I have walked in the Coliseum and heard the ghastly stories of what happened to the Christians of the early church there. Some they wrapped in animal skins and fed to dogs; others were turned into human torches and used to brighten their arenas. Today, we do things like threatening to leave our sanctuaries because someone changed the song service. I recently watched a sermon by Francis Chan in which he said to his congregation, "How many of you would stay here if I removed the pews? If I took the roof off?" Christians in Asia meet in caves by candlelight, and yet we won't go to church if we think the pastor is boring.

There was a time when our church was founded upon believers who counted themselves blessed if they could just share in the suffering of Christ. Let that sink in for a second. I have scolded God because I didn't get the raise I thought I deserved. Peter rejoiced after being beaten. Paul sang praises to God while in prison, while I have accused Him of abandonment because a book deal fell through.

The early church was built on light-bearers who refused to question God's goodness even in the face of a burning stake. Our current church has swallowed the myth that God is only present if we are rich, elevated, and distinguished. Do you not see the chasm? I seem to have fallen into it, and God is currently helping me as I fumble to brace myself.

Again, maybe God is not waiting on the world to become more naked. Maybe He has His eyes set on a generation that will wear nothing but the robes that come from His hands. Perhaps He refuses to lower His standards, and the Reformers set a high bar.

As Huss was fastened to the stake, he was asked once more if he would recant his messages. He was reminded one last time that if he would simply say that his ministry was in error, his life would be spared, and the fire would not be kindled.

Huss responded by saying, "What errors shall I renounce? I know myself guilty of none. I call God to witness that all that I have written and preached has been with the view of rescuing souls from sin and perdition; and, therefore, most joyfully will I confirm with my blood that truth which I have written and preached."

When the flames lifted around him, the onlookers reported that Huss began to sing, "Jesus, thou Son of David, have mercy on me."

Huss did not meet his death with screams of terror or cries for help. Instead, the sound of his song carried over the flames even while his body was burning, until the fire finally silenced the voice of the Reformer. When speaking of the persecution of the followers of Christ, Tertullian once wrote, "The oftener we are mown down by you, the more in number we grow; the blood of Christians is seed."*

With the early church their blood became seed. The more heroes died, the more followers arose. My question for us today is this: Is the life of Christians seed? We may not be having to die for our faith in twenty-first-century America. But are we even living for it? Or has this idea of feel-good Christianity so whitewashed our faith system that even a few sprinkles of rain casts us under shadows of doubt? The God we want to serve is the One who owns the cattle on a thousand hills. No one is chasing after the Jesus of Nazareth who was left hanging on a tree. That God is not as useful to us. The Jews didn't believe Jesus was Lord, because He didn't save them from their suffering and reestablish their reign over Rome. Does this at all sound familiar?

Satan's war tactics have hardly changed. He may have been around for millennia, but his arsenal is hardly new. If he can't get us trapped in sin, he will get us trapped in self. Heaven can keep the tortured Jesus with just twelve simple disciples. We want the miracle Jesus, the one who made the blind see and the lame walk. We will take that guy, as long as we can leave the other one behind. The one who said, "Foxes have holes and birds have

---

* Tertullian, *"Apology,"* in *Latin Christianity: Its Founder, Tertullian* (Ante-Nicene Fathers: The Writings of the Fathers Down to A.D. 325, vol. III) (Buffalo, NY: Christian Literature Company, 1885), 55.

nests, but the Son of Man has nowhere to lay his head," that guy is less appealing.

This is why there were only twelve disciples. The other onlookers heard Jesus say He had no home and turned on their heels. But surely Jesus couldn't have found twelve more devoted men. Most would later die for their ministry. He would hear the voices of His twelve comrades praising Him from their prison cells. He loved them, because they understood that there are two parts to discipleship. There was the God who made miracles, and the God who died by faith. They knew the segments were interchangeable, and they would follow Him anywhere. Perhaps God is not waiting for the world to get darker but for His church to regain its light.

I have been fascinated with reading literature on these great Reformers lately. Their deaths were as inspiring as their lives. I have been struck by the comparison between the Reformers and the apostles. Both groups suffered terrible persecution, and yet, when faced with the option to recant and move on, or hold tight to their teachings and be condemned, they rejoiced at the threshold of suffering.

First Peter 3:14 says, "But even if you should suffer for what is right, you are blessed. 'Do not fear their threats; do not be frightened.' " And Acts 5:41 says that the apostles left "rejoicing because they had been counted worthy of suffering disgrace" in the name of God.

I have been especially drawn to these church and scriptural leaders lately, because if there is one thing Christians can be sure of, it is that as time closes they will again meet suffering. Just as there was a message of truth that was met with persecution during the time of the apostles, and with Luther, Huss, and the Reformation, there will again be a message of truth that will be met with persecution in the last days. It is already happening in countries such as Sudan, where Christians are being beheaded today for their faith in Christ.

Right now in our world, there is pressure on Christians to accept human theories and doctrines over the unmovable Truth of Scripture. Under pressure to conform to the world in order to be accepted, even I have, at times, felt it better to keep quiet. I don't think I am alone. Christians everywhere are finding themselves in the middle of a great controversy. Do we follow in the footsteps of the apostles and Reformers before us? Or do we shrink into the shadows and distance ourselves from the Truth of God's Word? Many have chosen the latter.

Remember the words in your Bible found in John 15:19, 20. "If you belonged to the world, it would love you as its own. As it is, you do not belong to the world, but I have chosen you out of the world. That is why the world hates you. Remember what I told you: 'A servant is not greater than his master.' If they persecuted me, they will persecute you also."

The world is no more in harmony with the Word of God today than it was in the days of Christ or Huss. Satan has been ever diligent, mingling truth with lies, hoping that Christians will keep their mouths shut. In the parable of Matthew 25 we are reminded of what it will take in order to be counted worthy of the gates of heaven. We must be madly in love with our Savior, and we must hold tight to our Truth in Scripture. Countless people died not just because they were madly in love with Christ but also because they would not bend their conviction of His Truth. If you want to find Christ, you must find His Truth. If you want to find Truth, you must seek Christ. In John 14:6 Jesus said, "I am the way, the truth, and the life: no man cometh unto the Father, but by me" (KJV). If we are trying to find a way out of our nakedness, we have got to become convicted on the Truth found in Scripture.

Last, I will share with you the words of Jerome, who served faithfully beside Huss and was also led to the stake. When the executioner stepped forward, Jerome cried, "Come forward boldly; apply the fire before my face. Had I been afraid, I should not be here."

Jerome's last words, like those of Huss, were not the sobs of a man in pain or the panic of a man afraid, but rather the boldness of a man in faith. Before the fire silenced his voice, he said, "O Lord, Almighty Father, have pity on me, and pardon my sins; for thou knowest that I have always loved thy truth."

Jerome, Wycliffe, Huss, and the apostles met a death that rang true with those words of Tertullian, "the blood of Christians is seed." In fact, it is because of these great men that Satan had to change his war tactic. The more he killed them, the more they grew. Satan eventually decided that rather than attack the church as he had been doing, he would need to infiltrate it. And thus we find ourselves today with wolves in sheep's clothing, lovers of self more than lovers of truth.

No matter how hard Satan may try to drown you out or mow you down, cling tight to the feet of your Savior, especially as we near these last days. The devil will work vigorously to destroy us with bouts of suffering and prod us with pain. There is nothing we will endure that our Savior did not endure first. If only our eyes could see the angels standing guard around us and providing a hand to hold us up. The greatest gift of every Christian is the promise of eternity with Jesus.

When we embrace the worst of suffering, we can cry out that our Redeemer lives. We need not fear that which kills the body, for our souls rest in the hands of our Savior.

And so the apostles rejoiced, and Huss sang while he was burned at the stake. This is why we suffer: because Satan would rather rip off his ears than continue listening to the sound of our voices in praise. Real faith is not based on being clothed by blessings. Real faith stands still in nakedness. Remember, the command has already been given, Let there be light. Where light is, there God is also.

We are nearing the last days, and a time of trouble is about to close upon us like the setting of the evening sun. We are not to be afraid. Like Jerome, may we fight to the end. May the Lord know that we love His Truth.

Yes. The blood of true Christians is always seed, and their lives should be light on hills.

> *"If you belonged to the world, it would love you as its own. As it is, you do not belong to the world, but I have chosen you out of the world. That is why the world hates you. Remember what I told you: 'A servant is not greater than his master.' If they persecuted me, they will persecute you also" (John 15:19, 20).*

## Share the Naked Truth:

1. How does today's church relate to the church of the Reformers?

2. Will God actually come back if the church does not change?

3. In 140 characters, write a prayer for today's church. Tweet/Facebook us *@InLifeAfterEden.*

4. Or Instagram us a photo of your favorite highlighted quote from this reading.

## Day 16 — Seth

# A Hill Worth Dying On

Your battles inspired me—not the obvious material battles
but those that were fought and won behind your forehead.
—James Joyce

Ice hockey just might be one of the most brutal sports ever invented—grown men flying across the ice like circus performers only to collide head-on with the contesting team members in an all-out effort to gain control of the puck. Stan Mikita of the Chicago Black Hawks was no stranger to such spectacles. His career spanned the years 1959 to 1980. He was one of the meanest ice warriors of his day. He was known for spending a lot of time in the penalty box during his early career for unnecessary force. And then Stan was forced to rethink his game strategy when his eight-year-old daughter confronted him after one of his games.

She asked him, "Why do you spend so much time sitting down?"

Stan Mikita was one of those athletes who left his heart on the ice every time. Noted for his intensity when playing, Stan always gave it his all. His problem was that he often tried winning by engaging in unnecessary fights on the ice. He had to learn the hard way that knowing when to fight is half the battle.

I think that if we are honest with ourselves, we will find the story of Stan relevant to our own lives. I can't count how many times in my spiritual journey I have found myself stuck in the penalty box because of poor game strategy, and consequently losing the game entirely. I believe that the key to winning lies in choosing your battles, knowing that sometimes you'll fight and sometimes you won't.

I am reminded of the story in Genesis 32, where we find Jacob in the heat of his own battle that leaves him exhausted and injured. Yet it was one that Jacob weighed out and knew he had no choice but to fight. As far as Jacob was concerned, he was just hours away from dying at the hands of his vengeful brother, Esau. Before he came face to face with Esau he faced an even bigger challenge. In that moment, when Jacob felt the grip of God embrace him, he knew that this was one of those moments when you don't back down. He knew that his only hope was to collide head-on with God and never let go. Jacob understood strategy. In order to live through the encounter with his brother Esau, he must first let his encounter with God live through him.

In Genesis 25:29–34 we find Jacob as a young man, contemplating the promise given by the angel of the Lord. *The Seventh-day Adventist Bible Commentary* says, "Jacob knew of the angel's prophecy concerning himself and his brother, made prior to their birth." His strategy in this story was to literally take advantage of Esau's ravenous appetite. Cunning Jacob took his brother's birthright in a moment of starvation.

Reading on a few chapters in Genesis 27, we see this strategy once again evident in Jacob's life. Things heat up when Rebekah prompts Jacob to lie to his own father in the closing hours of his life. Placing the scented clothing and fur over his smooth skin, Jacob conceals his identity. Isaac is feeble, and his sight is gone. Jacob pushes forward in this plan to steal the blessing of his father through trickery. It works, but not without cost. Esau is furious, and upon receiving the news of what has happened, he vows to take revenge.

Jacob desired the win in life, but, like Stan Mikita, he went about it all wrong. His pattern of self-sufficiency eventually caught up with him. Fleeing from one place to another, Jacob must have had many occasions when he could hardly catch his breath from exhaustion. Can you relate? Has your life become one catastrophe after another? Self-induced affliction has to be one of the hardest lessons we have to learn in this life after Eden. I wonder how his younger years would read differently if he had chosen to wait upon the Lord instead of strategizing for himself.

Fast-forward a little farther in the Bible to Genesis 32, and we find

Jacob seeking one last time to use a strategy to save his own skin. He is about to meet Esau, and he is shaking in his sandals. So Jacob does something very interesting. He says to his servants, "Pass over before me and put some distance between successive droves" (Genesis 32:16, NKJV). He has them break into groups and sends them group by group. And Jacob says in verse 20, "I will appease him with a present that goes before me, and afterward I will see his face and perhaps he will accept me" (NKJV). Do you understand what Jacob has just done? Instead of sending all his men with the gifts of sheep, rams, camels, and so on, all at once, he sends them in sections. He will overwhelm Esau with what appears to be a larger number of gifts. Jacob, the master of strategy, always lives one calculated move ahead of his opponent.

I can remember waking up as a little boy and running to the Christmas tree to see how many gifts had my name on them. I would count them— one, two three, four . . . If I had been allowed to just have at it, I would have ripped all of them open at once. My presents would have lasted all of thirty seconds. My mother always methodically handed them out one by one to my brothers and me. What could have easily lasted thirty seconds took much longer. By doing it this way, she seemed to make the gifts never have an end. This was exactly what Jacob had in mind when he sent his men with successive droves.

But now, in Genesis 32:22–31, Jacob has finally come face to face with someone who couldn't be tricked or manipulated. Even his most crafty tactics are no match for his next opponent. No human-devised plan of preservation could get Jacob out of his next match-up. Jacob may have won a few encounters with humanity, but he was about to be crippled by the power and glory of divinity.

We find Jacob alone, purposely seeking something or someone. This is where the battle begins. And throughout the night, Jacob must decide his strategy. Will he hold on, or will he give up and let go? His entire life has been one struggle after another, literally holding on by a thread at times. This was the moment when God put the brakes on this wise guy.

Scripture says that this was no ordinary holy being, for Jacob himself refers to this "Man" as God. *The Seventh-day Adventist Bible Commentary* says that Jacob's purpose for being alone that night was to seek God in prayer. Harriet Beecher Stowe once said that when you get into a "tight place and everything goes against you, till it seems as though you could not hang on a minute longer, never give up then, for that is just the place and time that the tide will turn."

I remember the many times my daughter London squeezed my leg as I left for work. "Daddy, please don't go," she'd say. This is what God wants from us, as this is the moment that changes destiny. Anyone who clings to Him with physical desperation actually has the power to change the future.

When it comes to God, you only need one strategy. Hang on, and don't let go. Are you desperate for a change in your life? Do you need a way out from the string of messes that have caught up with you?

When I went back to college, I thought, "Where is the strategy in this? This is crazy." I was giving up my job and our family insurance, since I was the main provider. I tried to think it through, but I had no strategy. I wasn't even sure I was going to pass my classes. I had a horrible track record. Right after high school I had failed in college. Straight Fs. None of it made sense. I realized that I had to do one thing: hang on, and don't let go.

For some reason, our family always had just enough. I can remember one day when my wife was near tears because she was embarrassed that we couldn't make the mortgage. I felt so guilty. I wondered if I had made the right decision. Within an hour, my wife got an unexpected check in the mail. It was for the amount of our mortgage on the day it was due. In school, I went from straight Fs to As and Bs. I was even asked by a professor to be a tutor. I kept looking around to see if she was really talking to me.

A college degree wasn't something I could even strategize for. It always seemed out of reach to me. But something happens when we hold on to God and don't let go.

Jacob exclaims, "For I have seen God face to face, and my life is preserved" (Genesis 32:30).

Let your strategy this day be to see the face of God.

*"Devise your strategy, but it will be thwarted; propose your*
*plan, but it will not stand, for God is with us" (Isaiah 8:10).*

**Share the Naked Truth:**

1. In what ways can you relate to Jacob?

2. Tell about a time you held on to God when you didn't know what else to do.

3. In 140 characters, tell God your new strategy. Tweet/Facebook us *@InLifeAfterEden.*

4. Or Instagram us a photo of your favorite highlighted quote from this reading.

# But It Was Empty

I felt very still and empty, the way the eye of a tornado must
feel, moving dully along in the middle of the
surrounding hullabaloo.—Sylvia Plath

She fills her glass and hits the floor. The music blares. She rocks her hips
to the beat of the song she swore she'd never dance to. He had broken her
heart but did it slowly. The same way he used to undress her. So softly
she barely noticed. Every step she takes leaves a trail of dust. She swallows
hard, and it stings her throat. She smiles from the pain and prays for the
day that the only thing she can feel is numb.

Her friends said this would help her. The loud music and the smell of
sweat would make her feel alive again. She just wanted to feel alive again.
For seven months she'd taken her pulse daily and been surprised by the
thud every time. Good girls could be bad too. She didn't know what she
was doing, but she pretended to fit in. The scene was dark, and a haze of
smoke blurred her vision. She could get used to this, she thought.

At home, in twin-size beds, slept three children. After ten years of marriage, it would be the only thing he gave her that he never tried to take
back. She felt like a broken china doll, with edges so sharp you had to
handle them with care. Church secretary living in a glass house that was
always on display.

"You are so lucky to have him," people always said. The charming extro-
vert whom everyone had a picture with. She was always the shy, quiet type
behind the camera. Earlier that afternoon, she'd taken out their wedding

album. She flipped through the photographs and stained them with her tears. If only she had realized on the day, in her white dress, that ten years later she'd be wearing black. Her smile looked genuine, and her hair was tucked in place. These days she'd forgotten how to fake it, and the nights of stress had turned her gray.

She still slept on the right side. He liked to sprawl out, and so by habit she still slept thin. There was enough space in her king-size bed to fill all her memories. She tucked herself beside them and tried to drift back to sleep. Some mornings she still whispered his name. The silence pierced her ears. She'd smell his pillow and then hate herself for needing to. Somewhere across town slept the woman who'd replaced her. She envisioned his white shirt on someone else's floor, and she found herself dreaming of doing his laundry. People had always said that bad things don't happen to good people, and yet here she was, sleeping thin in an empty bed. Tonight, she'd be bad. Tonight, she'd give herself to the first person who would make her feel less lonely. She checked her pulse again.

The music blares, and she sees a stranger eyeing her across the room. She takes another sip from the glass she's filled, but all her lips can taste is empty.

\* \* \* \* \*

He's a loser and a spaz. If ever he has forgotten, the sign on his back is there to remind him. He lets the holes in his pants distract you from the holes in his heart. He slept on the lawn of his school once, and though the entire school knew, not one teacher asked him why. He got bounced around from normal classes to special ed to the juvenile center. It didn't matter that he could recite Robert Frost and Tolkien, because all they saw was long hair and dark clothes. He'd never be caught dead wearing color, because he couldn't relate to it. His world was as gray as his T-shirt.

He has slept on the couch for the past three days because he wants to hear his mother when she comes home. Two A.M. is closing time. He has an alarm to remind him, though he turns it off before it beeps. She stumbles in with a new man on her arm, and they laugh as they walk by the couch. He pretends to be sleeping, and she pretends she believes him. His stomach churns as they make their way up the stairs. If only she could glance in the mirror and see the image that he sees. She is beautiful without makeup, though her face is always painted in it. She's the only person who really gets him. She's the reason he believes that girls should be protected. In his eyes, her figure is translucent and her heart sits outside of her skin. She's the kindest, gentlest woman he knows, and so when a classmate called her sleazy, he fought for her honor. He lost, but he won her stripes. The visible battle wounds are far less painful than the hidden ones.

He thinks about the mat lying on their porch. "Welcome Home," it reads. He'd shred it in the morning. He was sick of people being "welcomed" here. That back door is revolving. When he dreams, he dreams that just for one night he could go to sleep without thinking of "2:00 A.M." He tiptoes to the cupboard to take one of his prescription pills. The doctor said he would sleep better, something to take the edge off. He cracks the lid, and, with watchdog eyes, he pops one into his mouth.

\* \* \* \* \*

She goes to bed at 8:00 P.M. She hopes if she brushes her teeth without being told and folds the laundry before they ask that maybe this family will keep her. She practiced her cute puppy face and worked overtime to earn their love. Love isn't free, you know. While other kids she knew worked for allowance or video games, she slaved away daily for affection. Anything to experience permanence. When she dreamed, she dreamed of statues. She envied how they could stand still.

The kids at school didn't understand why she guarded her desk like a warrior. How could they fully grasp what it felt like to finally see something with her name on it? When the teacher rearranged the classroom seating, she felt herself go into a panic. That desk was the one place she experienced stability. Third seat in, second row. That was the only address she had. If only she could receive mail there. She cried when suddenly she found that the desks' order had been changed. Mrs. Kush said it would be fun to try something new. That stopped being fun four houses, three twin-size beds, and one cot ago. The other kids started to laugh. Through tears she pushed it back into place and begged the teacher to let it be. Third seat in, second row, home sweet home.

She stares into the mirror and hopes that in the morning her hair will be less stringy. *If I could only be prettier,* she thinks to herself, *then someone would want me.* She uses the eraser of her pencil to try to rub out her freckles. When they ask her if she's hungry, she does her best to eat the food she has been given and then pretend she's full. She doesn't want to be expensive, she doesn't want to be a burden—she just wants to be wanted.

The woman wears lovely dresses, and the man drives a big truck. She envisions herself sipping tea with the woman in her own lovely dress someday and sitting and laughing with the man on the tailgate. Tonight when they fall asleep, she'll lift her pencil and scrub harder with the eraser. The food on her dinner plate is burned, but she swallows each bite anyway.

"It's delicious!" she squeals to the woman in the dress, and she swears she sees a smile. *It must be working,* she thinks while holding her breath. She scoops another burnt piece onto her fork and opens her mouth wide. She chews on it slowly. Large fork-sized scoops of empty.

\* \* \* \* \*

"Hosanna!" they scream while trampling over one another in the streets. They want to catch a glimpse of Him. They wave palm branches and feel the wind blowing joy through their hair.

"We love you!" some shout. Others call Him "king." The scene is picture-perfect, and the soldiers can't contain the mob.

He had told them that if they drank from His cup, they would never thirst again. He had promised that if they would connect to His Word, their vacant stares could be filled. They were naked, and He spoke of garments that would never leave them cold. They were hungry, and He preached of bread that would feed their bodies and their souls. He was the physical embodiment of life. His sacrifice would pave the way for a love so dense they could stop sinking and start swimming.

They keep singing His praises, and their adoration touches His heart. They keep begging to crown Him, but they can't quite get a handle on His kingdom. He smiles in their direction. He soaks up their accolades. He rides their donkey, holds their children, kisses their widows, and carries their burdens.

But He knows this moment will be short-lived. They can shout all they want, but in the echoes of their hearts, He sees that their words are empty.

*"May the God of hope fill you with all joy and peace as you trust in him, so that you may overflow with hope by the power of the Holy Spirit" (Romans 15:13).*

### Share the Naked Truth:

1. Are there any areas of your life that just feel empty?

2. How can you help someone else feel loved or acknowledged today?

3. In 140 characters, put a verse that you will share with others today in order to make them feel less empty. Tweet/Facebook us *@InLifeAfter Eden.*

4. Or Instagram us a photo of your favorite highlighted quote from this reading.

# Comatose

Sometimes it's the same moments that take your breath
away that breathe purpose and love back into your life.
—Steve Maraboli

I came across an article in the news this past week stating that three lives were saved in New York in just six days because CPR was administered at just the right moment. The story briefly described the three incidents, and they had one common thread: each survivor would have died within minutes if CPR had not resuscitated them.

We as Christians would face a fate similar to those resuscitated victims if Christ had not revived us. We too are stitched together by one common thread. It's the breath of life—the Holy Spirit. The problem is that many have been deprived of spiritual oxygen for so long that they've slipped into a coma-like state. We have allowed our minds to become altogether numb, unconsciously gasping for a source that is able to breathe life back into us once more.

It is through the acknowledgement of our need for the Holy Spirit that we gain spiritual resuscitation. For many, this life has become one stagnant day after another, while for others it is life on the verge of spiritual suffocation. They wish they could somehow overcome the emptiness and inner void.

It was the breath of God that went forth on the day Jesus cried out, "Lazarus, come forth!" (John 11:43, NKJV). We are told that immediately Lazarus arose from his physical sleep of death to a new life. God is calling you this day to come forth. He is clear that a transformation will start to take root within us. Everything else hinges on whether or not we have the Spirit in our lives.

Human beings are, to some extent, products of their environment. People who look as though they have had a rough life most likely have. As one of my good friends says, "They have a story. You can just tell." I think that sometimes the neglect from our earthly relationships spills over into our heavenly relationship, causing this invisible barrier between us and God.

Through the manifestation of sin we have morphed into these broken creatures that are no longer able to live up to their full potential because of the pain that has been wrought in their life. As a result, many people put up invisible fortresses around them—fortresses that have been created with their imagination.

I think you'd agree that the average person experiences some form of anxiety when somebody they don't trust or don't know gets physically too close to them. As human beings, we instinctively panic inside. Our heart rate increases, and we intuitively try to regain control of our invisible buffer zone. Inside, we question their motives and intent. We begin to ask ourselves, "Why are they so close?"

If we want more than a comatose life, one that looks more like living and less like dying, we need to have a Lazarus moment with God. We cannot do this without the breath of life. I do not care how much of the Bible you read, how many services you attend, or how much tithe you give, we cannot live as Christians without the baptism of the Holy Spirit. The disciples knew this, and so they were skeptical of accepting Gentiles until they found out that they had received not just the baptism of water but also the baptism of fire, which is the Holy Spirit. They didn't argue with the Spirit.

Sometimes survival looks like anything but surviving. This is why I believe that we can be alive and yet not be living. Picture with me, if you will, someone who is in a comatose state. Are they alive? Yes. Are they breathing? Yes. Are they living? Not really. They can't run, take a drink of water, sing a song, write a poem, laugh with their children, or love someone. They are comatose. Apart from the Spirit, we are comatose as well. We are barely breathing, unconscious to the true depths of what we were truly made for.

## Comatose

In the Old Testament, the prophet Ezekiel portrays with strong imagery a vision that God gave him.

> Also He said to me, "Prophesy to the breath, prophesy, son of man, and say to the breath, 'Thus says the Lord God: "Come from the four winds, O breath, and breathe on these slain, that they may live." ' " So I prophesied as He commanded me, and breath came into them, and they lived, and stood upon their feet, an exceedingly great army. Then He said to me, "Son of man, these bones are the whole house of Israel. They indeed say, 'Our bones are dry, our hope is lost, and we ourselves are cut off!' " (Ezekiel 37:9–11).

Israel had lost sight of God for what seemed to be the millionth time. Trusting in false gods and humans, they pushed aside the Creator's love for them. It didn't take long to see the result of their handiwork. Ezekiel portrays them as a valley of dry bones, a people who traded the glory of God for a life that was on the verge of physical and spiritual death. It was through God's grace that He prophesied using Ezekiel. He told Israel that although they were comatose, He would breathe this breath of life into them once more. And without the Holy Spirit, without a baptism of fire, we, too, are a valley of dry bones.

Scripture tells us that God "breathed into his nostrils the breath of life; and man became a living being" (Genesis 2:7). Life started with the breath of God in Eden, and when Christ cried out on the cross, "It is finished," He again gave us His breath and breathed life into our souls. In Genesis His breath awakens our bodies, and at the cross His last breath awakens our souls.

I think one of the biggest misconceptions in our church today is that we are living, and yet we look more like a valley of dry bones. The Bible is clear: when the breath of the Spirit comes upon you, supernatural things happen. If we are not experiencing the supernatural, perhaps it is because we are barely breathing.

I don't know about you, but I want to be baptized by fire. I want the breath of the Holy Spirit. I was not created to live comatose, and yet I find that I have gone through life resting in a valley of dry bones.

# Life After Eden

*"The Spirit of God has made me; the breath of the Almighty gives me life" (Job 33:4).*

## Share the Naked Truth:

1. Do our churches reflect a church with the breath of God? Why or why not?

2. What would we look like if we actually received the breath of the Holy Spirit? Would things look different?

3. In 140 characters, put a verse that displays a time the apostles clearly received the baptism of fire, and what that looked like. Tweet/Facebook us *@InLifeAfterEden.*

4. Or Instagram us a photo of your favorite highlighted quote from this reading.

# Day 19 — Heather

# Dear Adulterer

Christ and the Church: If he were to apply for a divorce on the grounds of cruelty, adultery and desertion, he would probably get one.—Samuel Butler

## An Open Letter

To Whom It May Concern:

When we met, My eyes danced around you. When you cast a look My way, I could barely breathe. You talked, and I listened. With each word your face brightened, and I almost had the feeling that in all your previous years, no one had ever heard you; not the way I did. Your lips moved, and waves in the background crashed, and right then in My bones I knew that you were a song I would have stuck in My head for the rest of My life. I loved you then. The feeling of adoration that I felt when you brought Me near you was almost indescribable. I wanted everyone to see that I was with you, and the sun seemed to shine a little brighter in those days. Did you feel warm in My rays?

I am not exactly sure what happened next. Apparently, for you, love was a feeling and not a choice. The second that things grew comfortable, I saw your eyes lingering in directions that were not mine. It stung. My heart burned with jealousy, but I bit My own fist in silence. I was dumbfounded. As My knuckles grew raw from My gnawing, you held them in one hand and poured salt on them with the other. You have become an acrobat with the truth—balancing lies like a tightrope walker. With every step I saw

123

betrayal. But I let you walk that line anyway.

You were young and foolish when I found you, and at My side you grew strong. People noticed. Suddenly you were something. Suddenly your name stopped being spoken like an afterthought, and when I wasn't the only hand you could reach out to, that's when you discovered your incredible knack for "balance."

You lost your grin of humility and became proud of your own beauty. You no longer stood taller when I was near you; your shoulders were straight without Me. Everyone acknowledged your strength and your beauty, and I saw you change toward Me. We talked, and I still hung on every word, but you no longer spoke as if you were waiting for My approval. You had found your own accolades, and My words lost their magic. Beneath the vanity and ego you were dressed in was a body standing naked.

Do you remember when I was your focus? You'd call for Me. In the middle of the night, when you should have been asleep, you were awake because you needed Me. There was a time when I was always your first call. There were days, distant days, when apologies weren't necessary. Then you walked that tightrope, and with each step of your foot, salt fell—more dressing for My wounds.

Suddenly our bed grew cold, and I lay awake most nights just hoping you would notice My eyes on you and ask if something was wrong. You didn't. I am not sure you could feel My gaze anymore. Not the way you used to. We used to finish each other's sentences. Now I'm preaching sermons to an empty pew. The skinny kid with glasses changed. I helped elevate you, and you flipped off the platform, leaving Me behind. They found you lovely, and you found their praise intriguing.

Our relationship became less and less about Me and more and more about you. You asked Me questions and left before I even gave an answer. You stayed out late with friends, and eventually you stopped coming home altogether. We never really talked about the distance that was growing between us. You just kept standing one foot farther away from Me each day. The heat turned up around us, but you never noticed the water getting warmer. Soon it will be boiling, and you will be sorry. This pot will scald you. On that day you will reach out for Me, and I wonder if it will be the first time you realize just how far away you've run from Me.

### Dear Adulterer

They keep telling you that life is about the pursuit of your happiness. They say I am a ball and chain that holds you back from chasing freedom. Grab your dreams; just do *you*; carpe diem! They are so broken in their own misery. You are naked lovers clinging to each other for warmth, but each body is colder than the last. While they fumble around in the dark with their tongues swollen and lips chapped, I see them desperate for a drink of water. True love is the only cup that will soothe them. The corners of their mouths crack.

You cheated on Me. You cheated on Me with yourself as, slowly but surely, you gratified your own needs and desires without a second thought for me. I loved you, and you destroyed us. I waited up for you, and you never came. You have made a mockery of the house we built, and you should know that I am angry. I am angry enough to confront this in a letter.

You will cry tomorrow. When the sun rises and you stretch your arms in the bed you've made, you will find a stranger beside you. Their arms will not hold you, and their ears will shrug off every word you bellow. Their eyes will not dance around you, and tomorrow you will feel the sting that I have felt as I watched you grow smaller and smaller, as your figure kept stepping farther and farther away from me. Tomorrow the salt from your steps will dash into your own set of wounds. Tomorrow your tightrope will snap, your balancing act will crumble, and the vanity you are clothed in will be stripped from your naked body.

You will cry tomorrow. But tonight, you will finish your beer. Tonight you will laugh with friends and admire yourself in the mirror. Tonight you will think that you are invincible. But what you will not see is the skin breaking around your lips. You will miss the obvious signs of dehydration. And as the night goes on, you will grow weaker. Your beauty will leave you, and your happiness will fade. You will morph back into the skinny kid that no one noticed. Tomorrow you will wake up thirsty, and your tears will parch you more.

But, until tomorrow, dear, you probably won't even realize how cold you are. The heat from My embrace has ceased to warm you long ago. My arms flailed for you, but you were gone. So grab your blankets. You will wrap yourself in layers, but your teeth will still chatter. Your hands will shake, and the tips of your fingers will grow numb to match the dullness of your heart. You will burn to feel My arms around you then. You will cry tomorrow, and when the first daylight breaks, I will still be singing your song.

Even after you have embarrassed Me, even after you have humiliated Me, even after you have strangled My heart in your bare hands, your now numb fingers will find it still beating for you. You have brought strangers into our bed, and yet, tomorrow, when you cry out to Me, my ears will still warm to you. Love is not a feeling for Me, it is a choice, and I will choose to love you until the day you stop breathing. If only you would call for Me. Do you remember how well you're balanced when on your knees?

So this is an open letter to a cheater and adulterer, a philanderer and whore. To whom it may concern: when you wake up in the morning and find yourself shivering, know that before you even cried to Me, I had already written this letter forgiving you. Darling, I forgive you. Please, come home.

But you will not read any of this until tomorrow.

~God

> "You're cheating on God. If all you want is your own way,
> flirting with the world every chance you get, you end up ene-
> mies of God and his way. And do you suppose God doesn't care?
> The proverb has it that 'he's a fiercely jealous lover.' And what
> he gives in love is far better than anything else you'll find. It's
> common knowledge that 'God goes against the willful proud;
> God gives grace to the willing humble' "
> (James 4:4–6, The Message).

**Share the Naked Truth:**

1. Have you been cheating on God?

2. Do you truly love God more than you love your romantic partner or your children? How do you know that you do or don't?

3. In 140 characters, write an apology to God, acknowledging something you have placed before Him. Tweet/Facebook us *@InLifeAfter Eden.*

4. Or Instagram us a photo of your favorite highlighted quote from this reading.

# Day 20 —Seth

# A Sinner's Touch

If one by one we counted people out / For the least sin, it wouldn't take us long / To get so we had no one left to live with. / For to be social is to be forgiving.—Robert Frost

In Matthew 18:21 we find Jesus teaching by word of parables. Peter approaches the Messiah and asks this question, "Lord, how often shall my brother sin against me, and I forgive him? Up to seven times?" (NKJV). Can't you just imagine outspoken Peter dancing in his own sandals with anticipation as Jesus opened His mouth to answer? Perhaps Peter thought he was being generous with the number seven. Jesus probably took a deep breath and exhaled slowly, breathing His patience all over Peter's life.

With eyes that defined true love, Jesus places His hand on Peter's shoulder, the way a parent does when they want their child to know that what they're about to say is extremely important. Jesus replies, "I do not say to you, up to seven times, but up to seventy times seven" (verse 22).

Have you ever stopped to thank Jesus for not giving you what you deserved? Romans 5 is one of the most descriptive texts that helps us understand what Jesus did for us. If I were a good man, I might consider dying for someone of value (Romans 5:7, 8), yet it was without restraint that Jesus walked upon this diseased planet and bled on behalf of a people that left His mangled corpse to rot on a tree. The passion that drove Him to become a sacrifice for the undeserving is a mystery.

Born into a world of sin, the Creator took the form of humanity as He entered this sphere. Fully dependent upon His mother's breast for survival, He risked everything upon His arrival. He was given the name Jesus, which in Hebrew is *Yeshua* and is translated as salvation, for "He will save His people from their sins" (Matthew 1:21, NKJV).

Perhaps this is what John was getting at when he proclaimed the entire gospel message in just three words: "God is love" (1 John 4:8). Looking at Jesus, it was easy to dismiss Him as just another teacher of the law. It was not through His physical appearance that salvation was made accessible. It was much more than that; it was the blood that coursed through His veins where life lay untapped. Many looked redemption directly in the eyes and refused to believe that this was the answer, that He was the one prophesied about thousands of years in advance. After all, if Jesus was really who He claimed to be, why did He never work a single miracle on His own behalf?

When Jesus was tempted by Satan in the desert, why didn't He prove to Satan that He could do the things he asked Him to do? How easy it would have been for Jesus to simply say the word and *poof*—a stone transforms into a fresh loaf of bread. How in the world would this have affected anything that He came to do? The answer is found by taking a step back from the story and looking at the entire battle from the beginning. More was at stake than just an empty belly for Jesus. This was a challenge of authority. To whom would Jesus yield in a moment of human weakness? If Jesus yielded, not only would He have listened to an instruction from Satan, but He would have broken the chain of reliance that bound Him so closely to His Father. For Jesus this would have been sin. And if He sinned, we wouldn't know the words *grace*, *love*, and *redemption*. This would have become Satan's kingdom officially. Forever.

Instead, Jesus wore the robe of humanity with honor, for He knew that something more than a meal in the stomach must quench His hunger. "It is written, Man shall not live by bread alone, but by every word that comes from the mouth of God" (Matthew 4:4). Clinging to the thought that He might someday spend eternity with us, Jesus defied the rules of human nature. Instead of giving in to the desires of the flesh, Jesus refused them, signifying that His mission was not in any way to serve Himself but to live as an example.

What strikes me perhaps in the most profound way of all is the thought that Jesus needed human interaction. If He was truly 100 percent human, then He must have hungered for human touch. John 1:14 tells us that in Jesus the Word became "flesh and dwelt among us" (NKJV). Which leads us to a story in the Bible where Jesus does something contradictory to common practice.

In Luke 7 we find Jesus shattering the barrier of social norm as He allows a woman to wipe His feet with her hair. This might not seem like a big deal, but she was deemed unclean, a sinner. Looking for help, she clung to the ankles of this Man. Pouring perfume all over His feet, she wept uncontrollably. I can just imagine what that scene must have looked like. Curled around His legs, forgetting what everyone else would think, she probably moaned with deep sorrow as the tears rolled off her cheeks and found their place. She got to literally rest on the feet of Jesus.

Jesus says to Simon, "You gave Me no kiss, but this woman has not ceased to kiss my feet since the time I came in" (Luke 7:45, NKJV). A few verses later, we find Jesus talking about His appreciation for her act: "for she loved much" (verse 47). Jesus was drawn to Mary Magdalene because she touched Him without restraint. The Pharisees condemned her, saying, "She is a sinner" (verse 39). And Jesus welcomed her, for she not only acknowledged Him as the Messiah, the "anointed one," but allowed His human need for touch to be fulfilled.

In studying the life of Christ there is no denying His humanity, but through His miracles and unconditional love there is no denying His divinity. Jesus came into this earth 100 percent human so that we can relate to Him, and through His miracles and departure Jesus left 100 percent divine so that we might obtain salvation through Him.

"Therefore, in all things He had to be made like His brethren, that He might be a merciful and faithful High Priest in things pertaining to God, to make propitiation for the sins of the people. For in that He Himself has suffered, being tempted, He is able to aid those who are tempted" (Hebrews 2:17, 18, NKJV).

Jesus walked among us as a man so that we can identify with Him. He died bearing the "iniquity of us all" (Isaiah 53:6, NKJV) in the hope that everyone would seize the opportunity to receive the gift of eternal life through Him. Mary Magdalene was touched by sin and heard that Jesus had the power to "cleanse us from all unrighteousness" (1 John 1:9,

NKJV). His appearance was that of a man, but His words were that of a Savior.

In desperation, she fell to her knees in the presence of Jesus, longing to be freed from the cycle of abandonment and shame. This sinner used her last ounce of strength to carry the remains of her soul to Jesus, collapsing to the ground in defeat. The stench of her sin made the ridiculing Pharisees sick to their stomachs. As she lathered Jesus' feet with costly oils, the fragrance began saturating the air.

Forgetting about what other people thought of her, Mary Magdalene found herself in what appeared to be another humiliating position. A woman who was sure that her sense of value had been spoiled now found herself face to face with eyes that claimed her worthy. She had encountered Jesus—the Man who would save her from her sins.

They told her she was unlovable, and yet Jesus loved her. They told her she was worthless, and yet Jesus saw precious value. They told her she was damaged and flawed and broken, and Jesus made her new. Our answer to restoration cannot be found in the works we do or the degrees we hold. It is not by the things we accomplish or the sins we abstain from. Our answer must be found through a divine process of grace. We must daily wrap our broken bodies around the ankles of Jesus and squeeze so tightly that we can barely breathe. The answer is discovered when you weep uncontrollably in His presence and profess Him as Lord of your life. Your answer right now is lying untapped, waiting for you to discover it.

I challenge you with this question: who do you surrender your authority to? This is the question that will determine the answer to your sin. This will determine whether or not you fall into your "nightly rituals" of committing familiar sin in this life after Eden. It will be the key to the transformation of your soul, a restoration of the heart. The very last verse of this story reads, "Your faith has saved you; go in peace" (Luke 7:50).

I know what you're thinking right now. "Yeah, but she physically saw Jesus. I don't have this privilege. It is a little awkward to get on my knees and pray to someone I can't see." Even better. Jesus said to His disciple, "Thomas, because you have seen Me, you have believed. Blessed are those who have not seen and yet have believed" (John 20:29, NKJV).

You might not have Jesus in human flesh, but He has given us the Holy

Spirit. If you reach out through the moaning of your tears and profess that you believe He can restore you, an extra blessing will be poured out on you. The hand of God is so big that it is able to take your sin and crush it in its palm. Those hands that have devoured your sin are the hands of Jesus. They are now forever scarred, signifying that although this may be your seventh strike at failure, you still have "seventy times seven" more chances in this life after Eden. We know all too well "a sinner's touch." May we also discover the touch of a Savior.

*"Your faith has saved you. Go in peace"*
*(Luke 7:50).*

### Share the Naked Truth:

1. Does Jesus' forgiveness really trump sin?

2. What are the steps we need to take in order to receive forgiveness?

3. In 140 characters, forgive someone who has hurt you. Tweet/Facebook us *@InLifeAfterEden.*

4. Or Instagram us a photo of your favorite highlighted quote from this reading.

## Day 21 — Heather

# God Is Not Coming Back to Save a Church

For God does not show favoritism.
—Romans 2:11

I have had a revelation that sadly should not have taken me nearly thirty years to learn. God is not coming back to save a church; He is coming back to save individuals.

I don't know about you, but I struggle with some issues that I see going on within my church denomination. In reading the writings of such Reformers as Luther and Huss, I have been blown away by their commitment to God's truth. I think the denominational divisions in our Christian community have caused me to feel separated. I had thought of many truths in Scripture as belonging to my own denomination, not realizing that it is God's truth. Apparently, even when dressed in my finest church attire, I am naked.

What I have observed within my own neck of the woods left me feeling concerned for the future of our world. There seems to be a perpetual temptation to water down Scripture and make what was once about service to God into service to us. We want a religion that says "no rules apply." And I keep thinking, "How can this be happening in *my* church?"

This past weekend, God responded to me by saying, "I am not coming back to save a church, Heather. I am coming back to save individuals. Your church is not My church, but your people are My people."

The church, my church, is made up of individual people. You can't become a certain denomination and get a free ticket to Glory Land. God is watching and assessing individual hearts. There are individuals within our world churches who are committed to preserving the light of God's truth as found in Scripture (regardless of denomination).

The tricky part is that Satan knows his Scripture probably better than we do. After all, he used it to try to confuse Christ while He prepared Himself in the desert. Satan can quote chapters and verses. We should remember that the next time we wipe dust off our Bibles. Jesus defeated Satan because He knew His Scripture better than Satan did.

Matthew 4 begins by saying, "Then Jesus was led up by the Spirit into the wilderness to be tempted by the devil. And when He had fasted forty days and forty nights, afterward He was hungry. Now when the tempter came to Him, he said, 'If You are the Son of God, command that these stones become bread' " (NKJV).

Something to note here is that Jesus doesn't go into the wilderness to be tempted. The Scripture makes sure to explain that Jesus was led by the Spirit into the wilderness. He was seeking solitude, to be alone with the Spirit. He was trying to put His heart in a place where He could fulfill His mission. He did not go looking for Satan; it was Satan who came looking for Him. Something else to note is that Satan himself shows up. Satan knows that this is not a time to send his minions to do his bidding. This is a showdown between the Creator of the universe and the one who seeks to establish his own rule. This is the King of kings versus the prince of darkness. This is a fight between the one who clothes and the one who disrobes.

The last time he faced man was in Eden. The pair were spotless and dressed in the glory of God. The world was perfect, and the humans were strong—fresh from the hand of their Father. Now, several thousand years have passed. The race has degenerated, and it is clear that they are no longer in Eden. Perhaps Satan assumes that if he can just catch Christ when He's weak, he will shame Him as he shamed Adam.

Jesus hasn't eaten in forty days and forty nights. He is human, and He is hungry. Satan knows one thing all too well about us—we are driven by our appetites. He tempts God with essentially the same test he tempted Adam and Eve with. When he issued this temptation in Genesis, the first Adam bit into it. But watch what the second Adam does. "But He answered and said, 'It is written, "Man shall not live by bread alone, but by every word that proceeds from the mouth of God" ' " (Matthew 4:4, NKJV).

This is no coincidence. Adam gave in to his carnal appetite, and Christ overcomes it. Right where we failed, Christ conquers. Where we have doomed ourselves to damnation, Christ covers us and offers salvation. Christ speaks back to Satan the same words He spoke to Israel while they wandered hungry in the wilderness. Apparently God believes that the only thing we can truly rely on in this world is Scripture, which we should spiritually feed on. It is the best cure for wandering in what feels like a barren wilderness.

Verses 5 and 6 read, "Then the devil took Him up into the holy city, set Him on the pinnacle of the temple, and said to Him, 'If You are the Son of God, throw Yourself down. For it is written: "He shall give His angels charge over you," and, "In their hands they shall bear you up, lest you dash your foot against a stone" ' " (NKJV).

In the first temptation, Jesus uses Scripture to thwart the adversary. He tells him that essentially He lives and breathes only by trusting the Word of God. In the second, Satan shows his knowledge of the Scriptures. He basically says, "Since You are talking about trust, if You really are who You say You are, then trust God to save You if You jump from here. Doesn't Scripture say that the real Son of man would be able to do such a thing?"

It should be noted that Satan could not force God to do anything. He could not force Jesus down the hill, and he could not force Him to turn rocks to bread. He could only entice, solicit, and persuade Him. Likewise with us, Satan cannot make us sin. He did not make Eve eat the apple; he spun words until he convinced her. Satan cannot force us to follow him; we must choose him.

Verse 7 reads, "Jesus answered him, 'It is also written: "Do not put the Lord your God to the test." ' " We see these words penned earlier in Deuteronomy 6:16, referencing the story found in Exodus 17. Again the Israelites are in the wilderness and they thirst. They are griping and quarreling, and Moses has heard them testing God's goodness by whispering among themselves, "Is the Lord not among us?"

God had already sent plagues to free them from Egypt, divided the waters of the Red Sea, and provided them with the symbol of Passover so they knew that He would redeem them. And yet, still they tested Him. They questioned in their present distress whether He was with them at all—despite everything they had just witnessed. Satan hoped that Jesus would likewise doubt whether God was still with Him. Instead, Jesus responds to the devil's taunts with the words of Scripture.

Now, placing Jesus on a high mountain, the devil makes his final case. He points out the beauty of earth. He displays the majesty of Creation, and then he crowns himself the king of it all. He insinuates that he is the prince of this world and that if Jesus would bow before him, he would give Him the entire world (Matthew 4:8, 9).

When a king defeats another king in battle, the kingdom goes to the victor. Satan, after dethroning Adam, had declared himself the ruler of earth. This is why Jesus had to be born on earth and live a life as the second Adam. He had to redeem us from the tricks of the serpent.

On that hill, the scene was captivating. Satan offered Christ a way out of the sure destruction He would meet if He followed the call of God. Satan promised to give Jesus the world without the work. This was surely Satan's finest temptation. The road Christ would walk to Calvary would be horrible and agonizing. He'd be whipped, abused, and spit upon; beaten within an inch of His life, and die a humiliating death on a cross. Jesus—fully God and fully human—must have looked upon this scene with righteous indignation.

He responds to Satan in verse 10: "Away from me, Satan! For it is written: 'Worship the Lord your God, and serve him only.' "

Jesus made His choice. He would redeem the world through suffering. He would walk the painful steps to Calvary and wear a crown of thorns. Satan had no luck in tempting Jesus. But he has better luck in tempting us. Christ says that we are successful if we walk in righteousness, peace, and obedience. Satan tells us that we must lie, cheat, and steal our way to the top. He brings us up on mountains and says that this job, this attractive woman or man, this wealth could all be ours if we just play by his rules. Nice guys finish last, and he can show us how to win. Our response should be an echo of our Savior's: "Get thee behind me, Satan. I will worship my Lord God, and it is Him I will serve."

When we do this, the results can be found in verse 11. "Then the devil left him, and angels came and attended him."

I don't think we will ever fully understand our ransom until we are standing beside the Redeemer in heaven. Only when we are able to see the glory and beauty of His throne, the obedience and love of the angels, and the pride and honor of the Father will we truly be able to recognize everything that Christ did for us. He did not *have* to leave heaven to be met on earth with such cruelty—He chose to.

Adam failed, and he was consumed by nakedness. God could have walked away. He could have blotted us out and started over. Truly, we never would have known the difference. But He doesn't do that. He inserts Himself in the very thicket of thorns Adam left us in, and He paid the ultimate price. I want to be in heaven mainly because I want to appropriately thank God for everything He has done for me. And I know that part of my getting there is committing myself to His Spirit.

My point is that, regardless of your denomination, God wants you to know His Word for yourself. God has not chosen people by churches. He chooses individuals who are committed to representing His truth. At the end of the day, the religion instituted by man cannot supersede what God put in place. This was the fire that burned in the belly of the first church Reformers. As Jerome burned at the stake, the last words he said were, "May they know that I have always loved thy Truth."

I think many of us today are either under pressure from secular society or from within our own denominations to bury certain scriptural truths. The Reformers died for those truths. Jesus used them to conquer Satan in the wilderness. I would like to be able to say that I have done better than to bury it.

John 4:24 says, "God is a Spirit: and they that worship him must worship in spirit and in truth" (KJV). God wants your love, but He also wants you to love His truth. The only way you can know His truth for yourself is to first know God and then study His Word for yourself. Trying to figure out life after Eden is all about connecting the dots between your personal relationship with Jesus and the Jesus you meet in Scripture. That's it. Start and end your day by always combining those two facets of connection, and you will be in the game.

We do know that as the last days approach, God will not rain His Spirit down on us until we are united. I used to think that it was going to be many people in my denomination uniting to bring Him back. Now I think—well, actually I *know* that it will be a band of individuals who have decided to be committed to loving His truth. His Spirit does not operate along party lines. He rains on individuals who are asking for it. That is what happened in the Reformation. And I believe the first Reformation initiated by Wycliffe and Luther was a shadow of the reformation to come that will be instituted by us.

At the end of the day, God is not coming back to save a specific church. He is coming back to save individuals who have formed their own personal relationship with Him and are committed at all costs to protecting and preserving His truth. As seen in the first Reformation, God's truth is offensive to some people. There will be many who want to continue in their own thinking and their own sin, and when presented with scriptural truth they will lash out and want nothing to do with you. No wonder Jesus says in Luke 7:23, "And blessed is the one who is not offended by me" (ESV).

It was vanity and idiocy that led me to assume that only my church held the individuals committed to truth. God told me in John 10:16, "I have other sheep that are not of this sheep pen. I must bring them also. They too will listen to my voice, and there shall be one flock and one shepherd."

When Elijah assumed that he was the only one struggling to preserve God's truth, God chastened him, saying in 1 Kings 19:18, "Yet I reserve seven thousand in Israel—all whose knees have not bowed down to Baal and whose mouths have not kissed him."

You are not alone. God has others all around the world, of all different denominations, whom He has called, just like you, to life at this very moment in earth's history to accomplish this great work. Let us pray to encourage one another that we may commit to worshiping Him in both Spirit and in truth.

It will not be easy. Satan is a rabid dog thrashing in a pen, knowing his time is short. He will come after you as he did the Reformers. I assure you that there is nothing Satan fears more than a lover of Christ and an avid reader of His Word.

Do not just pray; pray and read His Scripture. He needs you to make that commitment. The Bible changed everything in my life. I always loved God, but it was not until I read His Word that I encountered His Truth.

God is not coming back to save a church! He is coming back to save individuals who worship Him in spirit and in truth.

*"He told them, 'The harvest is plentiful, but the workers are few. Ask the Lord of the harvest, therefore, to send out workers into his harvest field' " (Luke 10:2).*

## Share the Naked Truth:

1. Do you believe God is coming back for more than just your church? How do you know?

2. What are two biblical truths you think every Christian needs to understand in order to fully understand salvation?

3. In 140 characters, write a prayer to fellow workers. Tweet/Facebook us *@InLifeAfterEden.*

4. Or Instagram us a photo of your favorite highlighted quote from this reading.

## Day 22 — Heather

# If I Were the Devil

A brave man is a man who dares to look the Devil
in the face and tell him he is a Devil.
—James A. Garfield

I recently listened to audio by Paul Harvey called, "If I Were the Devil." That recording, along with some of my reading of C. S. Lewis, got me wondering what would be my order of business if I were the devil . . . I'd attack marriage, because a healthy, God-centered marriage is humans' best chance at producing healthy, God-centered children. These children then become pillars in their communities, calling for *revival*—that infectious word that makes me grit my teeth and swirls my stomach with nausea.

If I could destroy the sanctity of marriage, I'd hardly have to spend as much energy on the children that those imploding marriages produce. I'd raise divorce rates. I'd tell married people that when things feel broken, they shouldn't bother to fix it, and remind them that they can spice up monogamy by including multiple partners. I'd make certain that they forget that their marriage on earth is supposed to be a symbol of the wedding to come. They're the bride in that relationship, and so I'd devour their chastity. They won't understand the definition of commitment; I'd make sure of it. If I could distort their vision of a loving earthly father, I could more readily disfigure their understanding of a heavenly one. Broken marriages almost always birth broken people. I'd have no choice but to destroy marriage—if I were the devil.

I'd continue promoting war, but only because I enjoy the smell of blood. It is dangerous for my mission when humans are cognizant of their mortality. Typically when death is visible, people search for the one Person I hope they never find. I actually would rather they continue posting "selfies" to their Instagram account, dancing to the music that I'll continue swearing has no influence on them, and partying their nights away. Let them focus on themselves and convince others of how incredibly awesome they are. The second they realize that something is missing, they'll start searching for how to fill that void. I'd much rather they make this earth their heaven—if I were the devil.

Speaking of parties, I'd keep their focus on any substance that has the power to alter their mind. I'd have them scream "*Carpe diem!*" and whisper that they "only live once." Of course, the truth is that they could live forever, but their need for instant gratification should pacify that reality, while all the days that they are "seizing" will be mine. If I can hook them to the IV of self-medication, I'd be making far fewer rounds. Once that controls them, I really don't have to. They'll self-destruct without me, and I can focus my energy on my more difficult clients. While they spend their time debating how many is too many, I'll keep laughing because all I really need is one. After all, it only takes a spark to get a fire going. I'll burn their houses down before they even smell smoke. Convincing them of that first puff, poke, or swallow would be my meaning of the word *glorious*—if I were the devil.

I'd persuade them that the Bible is no longer relevant. You see, it is the one piece of literature completely devoted to their true King. The turning of every page wields the power of His throne. I'd convince them that it's tedious and old-fashioned. I'd use my spider-like fingers to spin Truth into lies. I'd use it to twist the very character of God. I'd raise up so many separate denominations that they'd forget that it is the same Lord. I'd tell them that it is like a textbook—just skim and highlight, and they'll pass the test. I'd strike at the very heart of the Ten Commandments and disguise the guidelines of Christ's love for them and one another as simple rules and regulations that are no longer valid. You see, I would take the biggest testament for the Christian church, with all of its prophetic and archaeological evidence, and I'd make sure that the majority of the people who claim to be followers never read it in its entirety. Christ called it the

Bread of Life, so I want them to die of famine. If anyone quotes from it, I'll be sure to evoke anger in the name of intolerance. I'd make sure it collected dust—if I were the devil.

I'd divide the people into political parties that fight for the right to kill babies and get angry over aiding the poor. They'll be so caught up in the name of their affiliations that they won't even recognize the genius of what I've done. I'd get people very much involved with worship, except the idol to adore would be themselves. I'd tell them that the position of their body doesn't at all affect the way they pray. I'd encourage every carnal appetite, especially sexual, until I destroyed their very ability to connect with anyone—including themselves. I'd get girls to spend their energy focused on their bodies and tell boys that a little bit of pornography is not only gratifying but normal. I'd have them work more, spend more, take more, fight more, and do my best to convince them that this life has nothing to do with anything but figuring out how to make themselves happy. I'd move about in the shadows and hide in the darkness and convince them that the illusion of me is just a ruse. Because they'll meet me soon enough—if I were the devil.

Then, I'd slave tirelessly and work diligently to induce them to think that if God is real He wouldn't want them anyway. What would the epitome of holiness want with the filth they are? I'd swear to them that the answer is "nothing" and then try my best to hide His nail-scarred hands from their view. I'd divert their attention from His palms to my finger, and I'd remind them of their pasts and try to steal their future. Every time they opened the Bible, every time they stepped into a church, every time they got on their knees, I'd show them that long, bony finger, and I'd keep pointing—if I were the devil.

Last, I'd cry. I'd bite my nails, pull at my hair, pace in circles, and practice keeping a calm face that would be betrayed by the shaking of my knees. I'd be keenly aware that with each ticking of their clocks, I am one second closer to that day when these dreary clouds will be shredded by His blinding light. The Son of man will descend. I'd worry about the sight of the saints' graves bursting open. I'd have chewed my fingers nearly raw imagining the moment when even my wobbly knees will bend at the sight of the risen Christ. I'd dread the sound of my own voice, when my old swollen tongue would cry out that Jesus is Lord! I'd rather fall on my own sword—if I were the devil.

I'd work vigorously with each sunrise. My black heart would thud with each sunset. I'd be sweating as the last grains of sand squeezed through that hour glass. I'd recognize the signs trumpeting that there is simply not much time left, and then I'd silence every one of their alarms. I'd sing for you a lullaby—if I were the devil.

*"Be sober-minded; be watchful. Your adversary the devil prowls around like a roaring lion, seeking someone to devour" (1 Peter 5:8, ESV).*

## Share the Naked Truth:

1. What do you think is a key area of our lives that the devil focuses on to hurt us?

2. What is the best way we can have victory over the devil? Is there anything we can do?

3. In 140 characters, write a verse where God addresses the devil. Tweet/Facebook us *@InLifeAfterEden.*

4. Or Instagram us a photo of your favorite highlighted quote from this reading.

## Day 23 — Heather

# Heaven: Why Can't Everyone Go?

We may be surprised at the people we find in heaven.
God has a soft spot for sinners.
—Desmond Tutu

I recently had lunch with a friend of mine. Somehow we got into a theological discussion, and she asked a question that I have found myself asking. Perhaps you have too.

"Why can't everyone go to heaven?" She was asking because she seriously wanted to know. The thought that not everyone would one day be in heaven really bothered her. She thinks everyone should be able to be there, so why can't they?

"Every soul has beauty," she continued. "Sometimes I get really angry that these beautiful souls, with so much potential, could one day cease to exist. I just can't wrap my mind around it." She took another sip from her drink and stared out the window.

Immediately I smiled. I think she was feeling bad about herself for not having unquestioning faith in God's decisions. She knows not everyone will go to heaven, and so she wondered if her questioning God's verdict made her less of a disciple. I smiled immediately because I knew that if anything, this proved her heart was so closely wrapped to God's she could feel what He feels.

If you have not, even once, lost sleep over this thought, I think you may still be missing the key point of Christianity. We should be angry and frustrated and losing sleep because of how desperately we want everyone we know, and everyone we don't know, to join us in heaven. The taste of a relationship with Jesus should be so potent that we can't rest until every person around us has tasted it also. We should not be content to tune only our own chords to fall in line with His music. We should be frantic because the only thing that feels better than coming face-to-face with your Savior is leading someone else to Him.

For a long time I didn't get this. For a long time I could sleep burden-free because I knew that I loved Him. In fact, for most of my "Christian" experience I was completely and utterly happy because I was reading my Bible, I was cautious about my lifestyle, and I was certain that I knew Jesus.

You can imagine my surprise when I recently realized that you can know of Jesus without knowing Him. I knew who He was, and I could quote to you from Scripture and argue my theological foundations, but His heart and mine were severely disconnected. I truly believe that had Christ returned three years ago, He would have turned to me and whispered the words from Matthew 25:12, "Truly I tell you, I don't know you."

I recently assigned a journal entry to my students in which they had to share with me pieces of their "hidden selves." Now, they could take it in a light-hearted direction and say they "still watch *Power Rangers*" or that when they were eight years old they had a major crush on Topanga from *Boy Meets World*. The point was for them to practice self-disclosure, to share information they typically don't share. I didn't say it had to be heavy. And yet, out of two hundred papers, more than half of them were.

Probably 60 percent of my female students shared with me that they've spent years hating the face in the mirror. No matter how much weight they lose, they still feel fat. This is the culture we are raising our young girls in, which says beauty is what you see not what you do and boys just want girls who are beautiful. You have no idea how much I would love to change this cultural narrative. I tell my friends all the time, "If I walk away from a conversation and the person I leave is more impacted by my looks than my words, then I have missed my mark." I want to raise a generation of girls and boys who think this way. I dream of a world where we impress one another with our character and our minds are the sexiest thing we see.

When I was about eleven, the boys in my class made rankings of the prettiest girls. They listed us out one through twenty-something and then posted the list on the bathroom door. You have no idea how many days I prayed and hoped that just maybe I could see my name at the top of that list. I never did. It didn't matter to me that I was smart, it didn't matter to me that I could write beautiful poems, and it didn't matter that I was funny. I just wanted the boys to think I was pretty, and if they didn't, then I wasn't good enough.

I never did see myself as beautiful. My father constantly spoke of me as though I were a walking dream, but the eleven-year-old boys I went to school with didn't seem to see what he saw. Eventually I taught myself to stop caring. I had my fair share of bullies as a child, and so one of the defense mechanisms I learned was to stop caring about what other people said or thought. This line of thinking followed me into adulthood. I can remember going on a trip with my father. He was doing evangelism in Texas, and he brought me along to be his secretary.

"I don't really care about people," I told him. I didn't. It felt strange to say aloud, but I didn't. I lived in my head a lot, and I did what felt right to me regardless of how it made other people feel. I taught myself that in order to survive my childhood I had to stop loving people. Suddenly I was an eighteen-year-old kid who claimed to know God and love Him and yet could not have cared less about His people. Then I started recognizing that God loved people, and if I didn't also love people, He must not actually be living in me as I thought He was.

I started praying that He would have me see people as He sees them. I used to be one of the most judgmental people you could ever meet. Now, I honestly believe I could dig into the background of serial killers and come up with a reason to love them. I want to see the good in people, and I truly believe that there is so much good in the hearts that beat around us—we just don't take the time to search for it.

Since beginning to teach college, I meet many people each year, and I am constantly struck by how beautiful people are. No one wakes up and thinks, "I can't wait to be mean today." Just as, in the past, I had developed a tough exterior in order to survive, they develop bad habits in order to protect themselves. I truly believe that hurt people hurt people. The angrier we are with ourselves, the more we lash out at those around us. If we loved ourselves, we wouldn't be so threatened by one another's happiness.

The greatest gift you can give another human being is a sense of worthiness. That is what God gives to us. He sees our hearts before He sees our skin. He sees our minds before He sees our faces. He fights hard for us, because beneath this whirlwind of broken nakedness, He sees untapped beauty. He has to give each of us a chance to either break our bad habits or let them harden around us like clay. The choice is ours, but the hope is always that we will crack with beauty.

I read journal entries from young men in my classes telling me about the scars that have been left from their abusive fathers and alcoholic mothers. I read two entries from people saying that their parents have been diagnosed with schizophrenia, and while one student has a pile of letters written by his mother telling him how much she hates him, another conveyed that if she is being honest, she hates herself.

Every day, every single day, we pass by people and never stop to think or wonder what their lives are like. A student stopped to see me yesterday. She evaded my eyes almost the whole time she talked. I kept staring into hers anyway. "I have come to realize something about myself," she said. "I am so accustomed to failure that I am comfortable in it. Failure doesn't scare me, success does." Her words have lingered in my mind. What would my life be like if I feared trying to push myself? Hurt people hurt people.

Ever since the first journal entry assignment I gave to my first classroom, I can't stop wondering. I can't stop thinking about all these people with these terrible circumstances who are just trying to silence the pain from their broken childhood long enough to hear themselves whisper, "You are worth something."

I paused in my lecture yesterday and told each of my classes that they were valuable to me, that their lives meant something, and that the fact that they were sitting in this room pursuing higher education in the midst of so much baggage made them heroes. I told them that their lives mattered—and for some of them, it was the first time they had ever heard that. Imagine if the first time you heard that your life mattered was from a college instructor you see for an hour and a half twice a week.

I think we often forget that there are so many suffering people in this world. We get so bogged down by the tragedy in our own lives that we forget we aren't the only ones drowning. We forget that there are classrooms and malls and offices and streets filled with people who are still deciding whether or not they love themselves.

As my last class exited my room yesterday, one young man stayed behind.

"Thank you for what you said today." His was not the journal entry I was referring to in my speech on perseverance. In fact, I am not even sure he even turned his in.

"When people ask me where I grew up, I want to respond to them 'a bar.' " He looked me dead in the eyes and didn't flinch.

"But you are here now," I responded and returned his stare so he could know I meant what I had said earlier.

"Now I am here," he repeated and then picked up his bag and walked out of the room.

My friend loses sleep at night because it bothers her that there are such beautiful souls who could one day cease to exist. She loses sleep over it, and Jesus lost His life over it. What are you losing over it?

"Why can't everyone go to heaven?" she wonders.

"Why can't they?" I answered her. "God already died so that we could live. Now it is up to those who know Him to share Him with those who don't. Maybe everyone who doesn't know Him could go to heaven if everyone who did know Him started asking this same question."

The person who sits in the cubicle next to you may wear a fake smile every single day. The student you teach may have a hard time concentrating in class because they are afraid of the signal that it is time to go home. The customer you served, the lady at the bank, the janitor who cleans your office, or the boss you think you know, all may be suffering from the worst type of loneliness. It's the loneliness that has taught them not to let anyone too close for fear that they may figure out that they are anything but normal.

While some try desperately to stand out, many others would give anything to feel as though they had somewhere they fit in. If only we could relieve them of the stress of loneliness. If only we cared enough about the people around us to start penetrating, one by one, the hidden selves they exhaust themselves to hide. Jesus wants them, and if you don't care about the life of the person next to you—the person He loves so intensely it is maddening—then you do not know Him. You couldn't possibly.

There is a world out there that is dying while we sit in our church pews getting fat off the gospel. I don't think Jesus came to this earth to preach people into heaven, I think He came to love them there. Love is what heals broken hearts and calms the sting of suffering. Love is a game changer. Love is what took my hard and cold heart and slowly began to warm it. God is love, and love changes everything.

I wonder if when we get to heaven, Jesus will ask us where everyone else is? What if He says to me, "I put you there, to love them here. You missed the point."

I was born into a Christian household. I attended church school till the eighth grade. I listened to sermons, sat in chapels, read my Bible, and sang from my hymnal—so why am I just now realizing what it means to be a Christian after nearly thirty years of being one?

It is part of our job description to love one another to heaven. So why can't everyone be there?

*"Above all, love each other deeply, because love*
*covers over a multitude of sins."*
*1 Peter 4:8*

### Share the Naked Truth:

1. Why won't more people be in heaven?

2. Was there ever a point in your life when you knew of God but didn't really know Him?

3. In 140 characters, what is the greatest gift you think we can give the people we interact with daily? Tweet/Facebook us *@InLifeAfterEden*.

4. Or Instagram us a photo of your favorite highlighted quote from this reading.

## Day 24 — Seth

# Is God Enough? Part 1

Our duty is found in the revealed will of God in the Scriptures. Our trust must be in the sovereign will of God as He works in the ordinary circumstances of our daily lives for our good and His glory.—Jerry Bridges

Visiting the Grand Canyon is at the top of my bucket list. I can only imagine peering over the edge of that majestic crevasse. My legs become a little shaky as I approach the immense drop-off. I take in a breath of fresh air as my eyes feast on the grandeur sculpted before me. Shuffling my feet a little closer to the edge of the abyss, I swallow hard and then let out a huge belt of air. "H-E-L-L-O!" I yell and then listen as the canyon replies.

Like a trained parrot, it echoes with a hushed response, "H-E-L-L-O . . . LO . . . Lo . . . lo . . . lo." Loud enough for me to hear but not loud enough to wake the neighbors. Have you ever had a similar experience to this when it comes to your walk with God?

Let's face it. When it comes to understanding God, there are moments in this life after Eden that the Christian is left clawing at any thread of hope—moments when you call out to God waiting for Him to answer. Instead, you are left with the echoes from your own voice as it fades into dead silence. Have you ever prayed earnestly for God to shed light on what appears to be a forsaken situation? Have you ever begged Him for mercy because the pain at hand is unbearable? Have you ever struggled to the point where it takes everything you have just to get out of bed in the morning? Have you ever experienced days when going through the motions of life is all you have to give? These are the moments that cause every muscle in your stomach to twist with excruciating disgust—when a fellow believer, out of ignorance, pats you on the shoulder in an attempt to ease your pain and tosses you a "God has a reason" bouquet.

You cast a blank smile back, hoping this will prevent them from doing any further damage. Rough patches such as these come from what appears to be an absence of God's intervention in your life. In the heat of these tough battles, encouraging words from our friends fall flat in light of your personal struggle—what do they know?

These moments can bring confusion to your already questionable view of God. It's almost like pressing a finger directly into that gaping wound you're dealing with. These are the moments in this life after Eden when we enter our church pews afraid that the truth about our spiritual state will be exposed. We have become broken beings huddled in fetal positions. In our ears plays that song on repeat—"Is God Enough?"

B. M. Launderville once said, "The vine clings to the oak during the fiercest of storms. Although the violence of nature may uproot the oak, twining tendrils still cling to it. If the vine is on the side opposite the wind, the great oak is its protection; if it is on the exposed side, the tempest only presses it closer to the trunk. In some of the storms of life, God intervenes and shelters us; while in others He allows us to be exposed, so that we will be pressed more closely to Him."

In this life after Eden, we find ourselves at the most inconvenient times colliding head-on with that canyon of darkness. We are thrown into the heart of the storm. The force is great, and the blow is unlike anything we have ever experienced before. It's those moments that often end with the sound of a church door being shut. One of the core reasons people leave the church is personal hardships. Interestingly enough, if you ask a devout Christian when their relationship with God really began, many will answer, "A time of personal hardship."

In the book *Is God To Blame?* Gregory Boyd tells the story of Melanie, a very troubled middle-aged woman who became lost in her walk with God. Melanie had once been filled with a fire that shone as a witness to her church and community; then came something that shook Melanie's faith to the core, causing her to become lifeless. She became a walking corpse, going through the motions of life, all the while carrying the stench of a rotting faith that was eating her from the inside out. Every week she sat in her usual spot and listened to the preacher. She always left the exact same way she entered and wrestled with the same baggage she came in with.

Several years earlier, Melanie had gotten married to her wonderful husband. And being in her mid-thirties, she wanted to have a child desperately before her biological clock ran out. She longed deeply to experience the mother-child bond. She could only imagine what joy it would bring to her life. After three years of failing to conceive, she sought a well-known physician with the hope that he could provide answers to her crisis. They soon discovered that Melanie had zero chance of conception. With this news she left devastated, only to have her tears of sorrow replaced with ones of joy as she later became pregnant. She thought it was nothing short of a modern-day miracle.

At the delivery, everything went as expected. In the OB room, Melanie was just seconds away from holding her precious child. As the baby came out, the umbilical cord became entangled around its neck, suffocating the child to death. This is where Melanie's life took a turn for the worse. She couldn't escape the pain that haunted her like a bad dream.

Her tears are symbolic of so many Christians living today. Many of us know all too well that cold plunge into the great abyss of this life after Eden. What are you up against right now? Maybe you are at a crossroad in your life similar to Melanie's? If you have ever been faced with a circumstance similar to hers, I invite you to hear me out. If you have ever reached a point in life where you have cried so hard you swear you would never catch your breath again, I invite you to keep reading. If questions about God's love and character have ever been dangled over the fire of doubt, I invite you to keep listening. If you are seeking a logical answer as to why horrible things happen to good people, I invite you to press forward with me.

Together let's journey down the road of suffering, reconstructing our view of God along the way, exposing the cold, hard truth of where our nakedness has led us. I am convinced that the defining moments of Christianity often come when we call out to God in the midst of chaos and anguish.

Echoes of a lost Eden are rampant and filled with the moans of sufferers who come from all corners of the earth. We are in the midst of a devil's playground. Our decaying flesh is a result of sin. The devil licks our wounds with his slimy lies about our Redeemer. The lies roll off his tongue like premeditated murder, causing us to become self-proclaimed obituaries. His venom is extremely potent, and when he bites, he sinks those grimy fangs into us at our most vulnerable spots. He pollutes our view of God like a slow intoxication. With masterful lies he whispers ever so softly into our ears. Then, like a disease with no cure, our faith slowly dies until there is nothing left of us. This is the point at which many Christians head out the steeple doors with no intention of returning.

Scripture tells us that it was Lucifer's desire to place himself above God that led to his ultimate dismissal from heaven. We know that Lucifer was the "bearer of light" and was perfect in all his ways until he chose, by his own free will, to foster feelings of animosity toward the Godhead. It reads, "You were perfect in all your ways from the day you were created, till iniquity was found in you. . . . Your heart was lifted up because of your beauty; you corrupted your wisdom for the sake of your splendor" (Ezekiel 28:15, 17, NKJV). "For you have said in your heart: 'I will ascend into heaven, I will exalt my throne above the stars of God; I will also sit on the mount of congregation on the farthest sides of the north; I will be like the Most High' " (Isaiah 14:13, 14, NKJV).

Going back to the story of Melanie, we find her later seeking answers to her tragedy. She became angry with God after a close family friend (a religion teacher) counseled her by saying, "This is the will of God. God must be trying to teach you a lesson. God caused you to suffer. Perhaps when you figure out the lesson, He will bless you with another child."

This is one of the biggest lies about God that the devil feeds to us: that God has become this puppet master playing tragedy into our lives in order to teach us a lesson. Scripture tells us that God can work all things to the good of those who love Him. Bad things will happen to us, and God has the power to turn even the worst of situations around if we let Him, but He is not the designer of a sinful world. The devil has that role. And at times we are his accomplices.

David Bentley Hart wrote about God's nature in his book titled *The Doors of the Sea: Where Was God in the Tsunami?* He quoted an article written by an atheist saying that either God is good and not omnipotent or God is omnipotent and not good. The atheist goes on to explain that God can't be both. If He were, wouldn't He put an end to the suffering humanity endures every day? As a Christian, Hart does not agree with this statement.

Arthur Ashe was a legendary tennis player who played at Wimbledon. You can imagine his shock when this young, healthy star contracted AIDS from contaminated blood that he had received during a heart surgery in 1983. He received thousands of letters, and he recounted one from a fan that, of course, asked the question, "Why you?"

This was his response: "People who mean well will inquire of me whether I ever ask myself, in the face of my diseases, 'Why me?' I never do. If I ask 'Why me?' as I am assaulted by heart disease and AIDS, I must ask 'Why me?' about my blessings, and question my right to enjoy them. The morning after I won Wimbledon in 1975 I should have asked 'Why me?' and doubted that I deserved the victory. If I don't ask 'Why me?' after my victories, I cannot ask 'Why me?' after my setbacks and disasters."

*"She weeps bitterly in the night, her tears on her cheek. None of her lovers comfort her. All her friends lied to her; they have become her enemies" (Lamentations 1:2, CEB).*

## Share the Naked Truth:

1. Can a good God exist in a sinful world? Why or why not?

2. What has been an experience that left you wondering, "Why me?"

3. In 140 characters, write what struggle has made you wonder whether or not God is enough. Tweet/Facebook us *@InLifeAfterEden.*

4. Or Instagram us a photo of your favorite highlighted quote from this reading.

# The Night I Called Off My Wedding

*Here's the paradox. We can fully embrace God's love only
when we recognize how completely unworthy of it we are.*
—Ann Tatlock

I was twenty-four years old when I got married. We invited our closest friends and family to Clearwater Beach in Florida, where we said our vows on a dinner cruise on the Gulf of Mexico. Clearwater was an important place to me as a child—it is a destination that has become almost mythical to me. I spent nearly every spring break there visiting my grandparents' condo, and I have incredible memories of walking down the strip with my sister when I was fourteen years old. Sometimes a car filled with boys would drive by and honk at us and I'd blush, enjoying the attention. We would go fishing with my grandpa there. We had a special spot on the dock where he would take us. My grandfather passed away a few years ago, and though I have many priceless memories of his time with me, many of the best ones are of the three of us fishing on that dock.

When I was in high school, my parents allowed us to bring a friend. I can tell you now that there is nothing like being fifteen, lying on the beach with your best friend, listening to popular music, and creating fake identities for yourselves. We could be anyone we wanted to be on the sand of that beach, and no one would ever know it. I have incredible memories in Clearwater, Florida, a lifetime of memories. When I was going to marry the man of my dreams, I couldn't think of a better place to make a new memory.

In all honesty, my wedding wasn't so much about the day as it was about the man.

Whenever people ask me about my husband, I describe him this way: "He is literally the guy every father prays his little girl will find." Though his dirty laundry spread across the floor and bread crumbs on the counter remind me that he is far from perfect—if it weren't for those things, I think I'd forget. He is my knight in shining armor, my biggest fan, my best friend.

I first met Seth in the sixth grade, and the second I saw him I knew he was special. At eleven years old he would call me and ask me to meet him at the park, and I'd pedal my bike the two miles as fast as I could. We would laugh and hold hands while sitting on the swing set. My religious philosophies were immature at best, but I was certain that if heaven existed, it would include Seth Day and a pair of swings. If you read my diary in the sixth grade, you would see his name littered across nearly every page. In fact, my father read a page from that diary when he married us, and the words are as true now as they were then. I was madly in love with Seth. I couldn't picture my life going any other way.

I should pause here and tell you a bit about our love story. I reconnected with Seth on what felt like the most naked night of my life. I was twenty-one years old when I got engaged, and I was ecstatic. But I was twenty-two years old when I called off that same engagement—two months before the wedding—and I was devastated.

The night my engagement ended was probably the worst night of my entire life. The thoughts leading up to this decision kind of came out of nowhere. Our relationship wasn't perfect, or even healthy, but up until the moment it ended, the thought that I might actually not marry him hadn't entered my mind. That night, I had a conversation with my parents, and they expressed concerns about the upcoming nuptials. And when I thought about it, I realized that I had some concerns as well.

I knew I was too much of a coward to call it off on my own if that was what needed to be done, so I prayed to my Father in heaven and said something like this: "Lord, this is the person that I have chosen, but if he isn't the person that You have chosen for me, please end it."

Within two minutes of my saying "Amen," my phone rang. It was my amazing and yet not-so-amazing fiancé breaking up with me. Now I should tell you that we did break up on a regular basis. "Break up to make up" had kind of been our norm. But I knew this time it was not a coincidence. I knew without a doubt that God had just answered my prayer. I wasn't supposed to marry him. It was the end of a fairy tale.

I lay in my bed feeling lifeless that evening. My parents had gone out of town, and I didn't have the strength to tell them yet what had happened. I hadn't even called any of my friends because all of my friends were either in my wedding or were his friends too. I was feeling humiliated, and I could swear that the wedding dress hanging in my closet kept poking its head out and laughing at me.

And then my phone rang. I figured it was my fiancé calling to tell me that he was sorry, only I knew that this time there would be no getting back together. As my girl Taylor Swift would say, we were "never ever ever getting back together. Like ever." It was over. I answered my phone, and the voice on the other end was not my fiancé's; it was Seth Day.

Here is the strange part of this story (if you don't think it is bizarre enough). When I knew Seth in the sixth grade, I thought he was a total dreamboat. His family moved away after seventh grade, and I didn't see him again until my sophomore year of college, when I laid eyes on him for the first time as an adult (and I use that term loosely). Instantly I thought, *Great, still a babe.* So I wrote my number down on a piece of paper and handed it to him. Obviously, I am far more forward than any normal girl should be.

I waited and waited, and he never called me. Later I saw him walking on campus with a girl who was apparently his high school and then college girlfriend. I was slightly embarrassed, but then I figured it would be best if I pretended that the only reason I had given him my number was so we could catch up on old times. Surely not because he was a dreamboat. And not because I still had a crush on this kid from sixth grade. Because that would just be weird. So I did what any normal, sane girl would do who had just handed her number to a guy who clearly had a girlfriend. I screamed his name across campus and waved hysterically.

My thought process was that he would assume that surely no normal girl who liked him would hand him her number and then, when he didn't dial it, scream his name across campus in front of his girlfriend. Naturally this girl must just be incredibly friendly.

It seemed to work, and he smiled and waved back. I continued doing this for the rest of the semester, and periodically when we ran into each other, he asked questions about my life. Eventually I started dating the guy who would later become my fiancé, and my crush on Seth faded. I still thought he was a dreamboat, but I stopped frantically waving my arms in his direction . . . for the most part.

You can imagine my disbelief when my phone rang two years later, on the very night that I had prayed for God to intercede for me. Seth was finally calling—the guy I still thought was a total babe. He had saved my little piece of paper for two years. He and his girlfriend had broken up a year earlier. He said there were other days he had wanted to dial that faded number written on the crinkled paper, but he worried I would think it was weird he had saved it all that time. Naturally my mind raced back to my screaming and arm-waving incidents, and I thought maybe he had forgotten who he was dealing with.

He said he didn't know why he was calling, but he just felt like he should, at least once. He didn't know why, but I did—immediately. I didn't know at that moment that he would be my husband, but I did know that God was having mercy on me and sending me a friend. I told Seth that my fiancé and I were supposed to be getting married in two months and that we had just called off the wedding. Being the attentive man that he is, he offered to drive the two hours to visit me the next day. He did.

We sat at a beach and talked. I warned him that I'd probably cry a lot, and he said he didn't mind, but in those hours we spent together that evening, I didn't feel sad once. I felt confused and afraid, but I didn't feel sadness. Don't get me wrong, the sadness would come in full force in the following weeks and months, but for that first night, I got to ignore it all. I was able to bury my hands in sand and stare into the eyes of my sixth-grade friend. Somewhere in between the waves and the lump in my throat I even felt the hints of romance.

Two weeks later, on another beach night, he reached for my hand. I still haven't let it go. God had written for me my very own fairy tale.

Romance stopped being candlelit dinners and walks on the beach the second I gave birth to our daughter. Romance no longer meant new dresses and high heels. Somehow, after almost seven years together, it has morphed into something different. Somehow, in between the 2:00 A.M. dirty diapers and a stack of bills on the counter, romance became something else.

Romance looks a lot like cold pizza for breakfast and assembling baby cribs. It feels like running to the store at midnight because we are out of milk. From my view, romance sounds like whispers during nap time and looks like macaroni cards. People complain that marriage sucks the romance out of relationships, but I couldn't disagree with them more. Marriage has given birth to a different phase of romance. The kind that isn't just fleeting hopes but means resolved certainty. People say romance won't last. Maybe not their kind of romance, but the best kind, the real kind. If you want to live a love song, allow God into the story. Because it takes three to make a fairy tale.

I frequently read blogs and articles from people who say that God doesn't care who you marry, you just have to make a choice. Nothing sends my fingers pounding a keyboard more quickly. If there is one thing I know for certain, it is that God absolutely cares who you marry! There's no earthly decision you will ever make that will affect the course of your life more than the decision of who you choose to spend your life with. Your goals will be made or broken in the hands of the spouse you choose. From that decision you will create tiny people. If you don't think God cares or wants to be incredibly involved in that decision, you do not know Him that well yet. I have heard wonderful pastors and theologians say that God has no one in particular for you, and I just want to ask them where that line of thinking leads. If God isn't intimately involved in the biggest decision I will make in life, what exactly does God care about? I hate when people suck the love and tenderness out of God. Sorry, but my God is my daddy, and my daddy certainly was vocal in my marital pursuit.

I don't think I have ever experienced anything more romantic than knowing without a shadow of a doubt that my heavenly Father was guiding me in the selection of my earthly spouse.

I love the description of romance given in Song of Solomon 5:16. Here in this biblical book of wisdom literature we see that true love needs two ingredients. Solomon's bride says of her lover, "His mouth is most sweet: yea, he is altogether lovely. This is my beloved, and this is my friend" (KJV). Apparently the key to distinguishing true romance from a fleeting emotion is the ability to find yourself as entranced in the chemistry as you are in the friendship.

My husband is not just "altogether lovely"; he is also my best friend. He is my first thought when something either beautiful or tragic happens. He is the most beautiful face I have ever seen, and when I close my eyes, he is all I see.

A relationship must be based on chemistry *and* friendship. Bulldozing through one while clinging to the other will not give you the romance that lasts. It is because of chemistry and friendship that Song of Solomon 7:10 can read, "I am my beloved's, and his desire is toward me" (NKJV). His desires—sexual, spiritual, and mental—are toward her, because he understands the need for romance.

So don't listen to the critics and skeptics who tell you that love in marriage does not last and that romance is not a necessity. Remember the song of the man who prayed for wisdom and to whom wisdom was granted. Remember that Song of Solomon 8:7 reads, "Many waters cannot quench love, nor can the floods drown it" (NKJV). Love is powerful. These lines of poetry sure sound a lot like romance to me. But please, of all the things that you remember, let this be the most important: if you want to live a love song, you must allow God into the story. Because it really does take three to make a fairy tale.

For our wedding, Seth and I wrote our own vows. When he recited his vows to me on March 6, 2011, he cried, and I loved him even more for it. He is the love of my life and the father of my children. He is my financial provider, my protector, my best friend, and my confidante. He is my groom, my husband.

I am often struck by the image the Bible provides in depicting Christ as the Groom and we His people as the bride. Christ is returning to collect His bride, but how will He find her? Is she waiting? Is she sitting at her window day and night anticipating the return of the love of her life? Has she been faithful while her Groom was away? Has she left the porch light on so that when He comes, He knows she's not forgotten Him? Has she loved Him even still? Or will He come knocking at the door, excited to see her, only to find that no one is home, or worse, with another man is in His bed? We are the bride, and as the bridegroom prepares His return, I have to ask, how will He find us?

Paul writes to the Corinthian church, "I am jealous for you with a godly jealousy. I promised you to one husband, to Christ, so that I might present you as a pure virgin to him" (2 Corinthians 11:2). What does Paul mean when he writes that we are to be "virgins" awaiting Christ's return? Ephesians 5:25–27 explains this imagery by saying, "Husbands, love your wives, just as Christ loved the church and gave himself up for her to make her holy, cleansing her by the washing with water through the word, and to present her to himself as a radiant church, without stain or wrinkle or any other blemish, but holy and blameless."

In Bible times, there was a period between when the bridegroom had selected his bride and the official marriage. That period of time was called betrothal. During the betrothal, all communication between the bride and her groom was carried on through the friend of the bridegroom. The friend of the bridegroom could also be the person who, knowing intimately the family of the groom, was able to select the perfect bride.

This is why John the Baptist says, "The bride belongs to the bridegroom. The friend who attends the bridegroom waits and listens for him, and is full of joy when he hears the bridegroom's voice. That joy is mine, and it is now complete" (John 3:29). You see, the Jews had been asking John the Baptist if he was the Messiah they had been waiting for, and in his response to them he claims the role of friend to the bridegroom. In other words, he is simply the friend of Jesus who is trying desperately to prepare the church for Christ's ministry. Today, not only are we going to be the bride of Christ in His second advent, but we are also able to act as the friend of the Bridegroom. It is our responsibility to prepare our friends, neighbors, and loved ones for the return of the Groom.

The betrothal period was much more serious than our modern engagement period—at that time you would need a certificate of divorce in order not to go through with the marriage. To cheat on your groom during betrothal was a grave sin, punishable by death. Since the crucifixion of Christ, the church has been in the betrothal period. We are supposed to be anxiously awaiting the return of Jesus. We are supposed to be at our windows keeping watch and listening for the sound of His footsteps. We are supposed to be looking in the mirror, checking ourselves over, making sure that on the most important day of our lives, we are at our best. We are supposed to be preparing ourselves for a wedding. But are we?

The truth is, we cannot anxiously await the return of a groom we do not love, and we cannot love a groom we do not know. We must seek to know Jesus—and to know Him is to love Him.

I fell madly in love with Seth because the more I knew him, the more I understood how blessed I was that he wanted me. I know that my husband is not perfect. There have been moments in my marriage when he has let me down, and I knew that would happen when I said, "I do." But I was still anxious to marry him. How much more anxious should we be to marry the God of heaven? Christ will never let us down. He is perfect. He is not just supposed to be the love of our lives but the Father of our children. He is our Provider, our Protector, and should be our Best Friend and our Confidante. He is our Groom; our Husband. It is only in a relationship with Him that we are able to walk through life feeling less naked.

Jesus made a plan for your destiny before you were even a thought in your mother's mind. He has loved us before we existed, and with His dying breath He exclaimed through action the sweetest marriage proposal ever heard. Knowing all your imperfections, knowing all your idiosyncrasies, knowing all the times you and I would let Him down, He still allowed Himself to be beaten and placed on two beams of wood. He died there, a sacrifice of love. I'm willing to bet that the only thing that kept His wrists secure as they drove in each nail was the thought of your face. And the thought that just maybe, when He returned and made the walk up your driveway, He would find you at the window, waiting.

"And at midnight a cry was heard: 'Behold, the bridegroom is coming' " (Matthew 25:6). Each time I turn on the news I am reminded that Jesus is coming. Every headline of murder, genocide, bombings, terrorism, and all the hate that infiltrates our human nature is a sign that this world is painfully naked and that the Bridegroom is coming. Surely a loud cry will be heard, "Behold, the bridegroom cometh!" But when He comes, how will He find us? My prayer is that He will find every reader of this book waiting, with their cups overflowing with oil, because they decided on this very page that they would cover their nakedness with the blood of Jesus.

> *"And at midnight a cry was heard: 'Behold, the bridegroom is coming'"* (Matthew 25:6).

## Share the Naked Truth:

1. How do you think you show the universe that you are waiting for Christ?

2. Are you married to Christ or dating Him?

3. In 140 characters, write a wedding vow to God. Tweet/Facebook us *@InLifeAfterEden.*

4. Or Instagram us a photo of your favorite highlighted quote from this reading.

# Is God Enough? Part 2: Being a Martyr

If God be our God, he will . . . give us peace in trouble:
when a storm without, he will make music within. The
world can create trouble in peace, but God can create
peace in trouble.—Thomas Watson

Picking up where we left off on Day 24, let's take a look at where God's character was initially put into question. Lucifer, the "bearer of light," was perfect in all his ways till he chose to foster feelings of animosity toward the Godhead. Lucifer deliberately chose to attempt the act of placing himself above the authority and rule of God. Based on Scripture, I believe God gave Lucifer the same opportunity that He gives each of us to turn away from our erring ways. Since sin was an "undiscovered" experience and emotion for him, I favor the thought that God didn't cast Lucifer beyond the realm of heaven without many heart-to-heart conversations about the destruction his decision would ultimately cause. When Lucifer held firm to his new thoughts, it left God with no choice but to cast him from heaven.

Lucifer, by his God-given ability to freely make his own choice, turned his back on the Creator and Sustainer of life. "And war broke out in heaven. Michael and his angels fought with the dragon; and the dragon and his angels fought" (Revelation 12:7). He ultimately veered from the light that kept heaven running efficiently through the ages. Scripture tells us that God had no choice but to cast Lucifer out of heaven.

This is where the battle began, and ever since, the devil has been enraged with God. Peter wrote, "Be sober, be vigilant; because your adversary the devil walks about like a roaring lion, seeking whomever he may devour" (1 Peter 5:8, NKJV). And he isn't alone, Scripture tells us in Revelation 12:4: "His tail swept away one-third of the stars in the sky, and he threw them to the earth" (NKJV). In Scripture, the word *stars* within a prophetic context means angels. So one-third of the angels are helping him.

The devil hates God and uses us like pawns in this war, because he knows it is only a matter of time before Jesus Christ returns to take His faithful to be with Him. He fills our lives with lie after lie about the character of God. In our weakest moments, he whispers questions in our ears: "If God loves you, why would He allow you to suffer so deeply? If God is all-powerful, why didn't He heal your brother from cancer? If God loves you, why did He allow your dad to beat your mother?" All his lies imply the question that resonates in our mind at some point in our journey of faith: Is God enough?

The devil has deceived God's children on more than one occasion. But today, let's set the record straight. We are told in Scripture that the devil brings death and Jesus brings life. John 10:10 reads, "The thief does not come except to steal, and to kill, and to destroy. I have come that they may have life, and that they may have it more abundantly" (NKJV). God hates suffering! His mission was to bring life to all who accepted Him, to rescue humankind from death and misery.

Often we think of God the Father in this same manner: a God of destruction, a God of anger, a God who sends tragedy into our lives for the sake of teaching us a lesson. When it comes to our depiction of Jesus, we see Him as a merciful intercessor saving us from God's eternal wrath—the God of condemnation, the God of suffering, the God who might not be enough. However, Jesus said, "He who has seen Me has seen the Father" (John 14:9, NKJV). He is a direct reflection of God the Father.

By spending time with Jesus, we come to know God the Father through the Holy Spirit. So let's take a moment to look at Jesus in order to reconstruct our view of God the Father. We are told in John 8:12 that Jesus is the "light of the world" and that through Him we may have direction in moments of confusion and suffering. John 6:35 tells us that in a dying world Jesus is "the bread of life," that anyone who comes to Him may never hunger or thirst again.

If Jesus comes to bring life, the Father must also be a giver of life. If God is good, why so much suffering? Is it simply that He is not powerful enough to end the suffering in our lives? Hart's book *The Doors of the Sea: Where Was God in the Tsunami?* explores this question. Hart writes: "Unless one can see the beginning and end of all things, unless one possesses a divine, eternal vantage upon all of time, unless one knows the precise nature of the relation between divine and created freedom, unless indeed one can fathom *infinite* wisdom, one can draw no conclusions from finite experience regarding the coincidence in God of omnipotence and perfect goodness."

Oftentimes we see suffering and think that we can simply put God into a box. God is both good and omnipotent. We think that we can strip Him of His goodness and power by allowing ourselves to live under the false pretense that we fully understand everything about Him.

How in the world can we attempt to place God's infinite wisdom into ours? Impossible. And yet we repeatedly seek to solve the mysteries of God by using our wisdom and understanding. We try to explain away all the mysteries of an omnipotent, glorious Creator. When we fail, which is inevitable, we point the finger and say, "God is to blame." But the truth is that God is love. C. S. Lewis explained it by saying that life is a linear timeline we can only see in the here and now, but God sees everything. We are stuck struggling in this rut of a life with a rudimentary understanding of how God operates.

Lewis goes on to explain in his book *The Problem of Pain* that when you "try to exclude the possibility of suffering which the order of nature and the existence of free wills involve, . . . you find that you have excluded life itself."* We still have life, this life after Eden. It is anything but ideal. The last thing God wants to do is cause His children to suffer. Since the fall of humanity, sin has ravished our souls, leaving its stamp on everything in this world. The freedom to choose is the essence of life. When Adam and Eve swallowed the lies of the devil, sin was unleashed. The knowledge of good and evil was no longer bound to a tree; the seeds took root in every living thing God ever created on this sphere.

When a little girl gets raped, we blame God. When someone walks into

* C. S. Lewis, *The Problem of Pain* (New York: HarperOne, 1996), 25.

a school and shoots up a room full of kindergartners, we blame God. But if God turned every wicked person to a heaping pile of ashes as soon as they were about to commit a heinous crime, everyone would no longer follow God out of love, but instead they would follow out of fear. This would go against the very character of God. He only desires obedience when love is the driving force, not the fear of annihilation. That is true love. The idea of forced obedience is not in God's handbook. In no way, shape, or form has He ever operated in such a way—and He never will.

Darrell Johnson tells us in his book *Experiencing the Trinity* the truth about the Father that is revealed through His relationship with His Son. He says, "The Father trusts the Son so much that he gave him the weight of the grand enterprise of salvation. And the Son trusts the Father so much that he went to the cross knowing it was the way to accomplish salvation."*

Lies about God causing suffering are put to rest at the Cross. Jesus became the means of ending suffering by becoming the ultimate sacrifice for our salvation. At the Cross we find our answer that God is enough! Through the suffering of the Son we see the love of God unleashed without restraint—for us. By looking at the Cross we see a clear depiction of the suffering of Jesus our Savior. He said, " 'Now My soul is troubled, and what shall I say? "Father, save Me from this hour"? But for this purpose I came to this hour. Father, glorify Your name.' Then a voice came from heaven saying, 'I have both glorified it and will glorify it again' " (John 12:27, 28, NKJV). On Calvary, Jesus pressed your face into the palms of His hands and whispered through the groan of tears, "I am enough."

While you suffer deeply in this life after Eden, He is enough. When cancer strikes your family, He is enough. His sacrifice was enough to end sin. Satan created suffering, and through the Cross Christ created a way out of it. He was enough. He will be enough. He is enough. This world will surely bring us trouble, but we can take heart, for He has overcome the world.

Our suffering serves a great purpose, although our finite minds can't understand every mystery. We can rest in the knowledge that someday God will put an end to suffering. The cross was enough to bridge the gap

---

* Darrell W. Johnson, *Experiencing the Trinity* (Vancouver, BC: Regent College Publishing, 2002), 66.

between heaven and earth. When we suffer, we can be confident in the Victor's presence. Through it, we can do the same thing Jesus did—claim the victory. The sole purpose of our existence is to glorify His name. Every time we fall to our knees and say through our suffering, "God, You are enough," we become partakers in the suffering of Christ. For God is love. And at Calvary, when faced with heartache and death, Jesus proved that His love was enough.

"Beloved, do not think it strange concerning the fiery trial which is to try you, as though some strange thing happened to you; but rejoice to the extent that you partake of Christ's suffering, that when His glory is revealed, you may also be glad with exceeding joy" (1 Peter 4:12, 13, NKJV).

My high school Bible teacher is what I like to call a modern-day hero of the faith. He's a man who came head-on with the sting this world delivers and never renounced his faith. Diagnosed with Lou Gehrig's disease, he eventually died with no question of where he stood. I can never forget hearing the story his daughter Kelley told after his passing. One day, during the last few months of his life, he was in the kitchen struggling to spread mustard on a piece of bread when it occurred to Kelley that her daddy didn't have long to live. She blurted out, *"Aren't you scared?"* and instantly wished she could take it back.

Without hesitation he replied, "Kelley, God knows what He is doing." That is how the glory of God is revealed through our suffering.

In an attempt to make God fade from the forefront of our minds, Satan orchestrated suffering. He is the creator, the designer, and the lover of suffering. I have noticed that the one key element that creates the difference between a terrible story and a victory is the attitude of the participant. I have heard and seen God turn the most painful, shocking, debilitating stories into testimonies. That is what my high school Bible teacher allowed God to do.

If you want to really understand this for yourself, then I challenge you to find the nearest football field where you live. You will need two things: yourself and a ballpoint pen. Walk to the center of that field and stick the butt of the pen into the center of that field. Leave it there and climb to the highest vantage point possible. Look around at the vastness of the field, and then focus on the almost invisible point on the tip of the pen. That ballpoint pen represents our finite wisdom and understanding as a fallen race, while the rest of the field is what God sees.

> *The LORD is close to the brokenhearted and saves*
> *those who are crushed in spirit (Psalm 34:18).*

**Share the Naked Truth:**

1. Is God enough?

2. Have you ever seen someone in suffering and yet still proclaiming God is good?

3. In 140 characters, answer whether or not suffering is enough to separate you from God? Tweet/Facebook us *@InLifeAfterEden.*

4. Or Instagram us a photo of your favorite highlighted quote from this reading.

# Secret Admirer

God will not permit any troubles to come upon us, unless
he has a specific plan by which great blessing can come out
of the difficulty.—Peter Marshall

In the fourth grade I received a letter from a secret admirer. I couldn't
breathe. It said something about how pretty and funny I was, and that
they loved my "fluffy" hair. Note here that if you ever get a secret admirer
letter describing your hair as "fluffy," this is probably not going to end
well. My admirer said he was too shy to tell me who he was but wanted
me to know that he thought I was special. At the end of the letter it asked
me to write him back. The instructions said something like, "Please put
your response in a bottle and leave it by the farthest end of the fence after
school." And so I did. I wrote back saying that I appreciated the kind
words and that he didn't have to be afraid to tell me who he was. I had
my hopes about who could have written this letter. There were a couple of
boys in my class who I couldn't help but dream had been the orchestrators
of this adorable manifestation of childhood romance.

I was not allowed to have a boyfriend. My parents both made that
very clear. But they couldn't stop me from having a crush on whomever I
wanted, or in this case, a secret admirer. My admirer and I corresponded
daily throughout the week. I'd find notes in my desk, and I continued
leaving bottles at the far end of the fence.

I don't know what it is about girls, but there really is nothing like the
feeling of knowing that someone else is thinking you're special. We have to

learn how to keep this need for attention and flattery in check, because it causes so many problems later in life. I can't tell you all the stupid mistakes I made in my life before I learned this valuable life lesson. You want a man to stand by your side one day, but you don't want to need a man. There is a big difference between *want* and *need*. Wanting is a normal human emotion, but needing places us in a position where we do desperate things to fill a void. In communications theory we say that power follows the principle of least interest. Whoever needs the relationship more places himself or herself in an inferior position in the relationship. By needing people, not wanting them, we actually lose power in our lives.

At some point the next week, I received my last letter from my secret admirer. He asked if we could meet and said that I could find him at the far end of the fence after school, where I had been leaving all my bottled-up letters. I went to the fence, and he never showed up. I waited, looking around anxiously, but I never saw anyone. I figured perhaps he had gotten too nervous, or maybe his mother had picked him up earlier than he anticipated. The next day I found out why he had not come. Essentially, he didn't exist.

A group of girls in my class had made him up and had been writing me the daily notes, and reading the letters I had written back. I was mortified. They were laughing when they explained their prank to me. I am not sure if they thought that I would think it equally as funny as they would, or if they wanted to see me cry—probably a mixture of both. Those were the days that I went home and got wrapped in the arms of my parents. "They're just jealous," my mother would say. That's what my mother always told me when mean schoolyard bullies made their presence known in my life. It was sweet of her to think that jealousy was the cause of my every female battle.

Often when I speak at women's retreats, I use illustrations from my childhood. Every time I share one of my stories, the entire room gasps. They can hardly believe I would be the holder of so many ugly memories. "But why in the world would kids not like you?" they ask me, genuinely confused. I think people forget that behind every grown woman was a not-as-polished little girl.

I realize now that often a lot of the problem was me. To be honest, I think for a long time I was a difficult person to like. I was extremely opinionated and hadn't yet learned that it's always best to save your thoughts for those who ask to hear them. Back then, if I thought you were wrong, I told you. If I thought you didn't understand something, I felt it quite important that I correct you. I wasn't always very nice either. Whatever thought popped into my head I figured should be said aloud. How mad or hurt could I be by those girls when in other moments in my life I had been that girl? So as I tell the women when I am speaking, if you have pity, don't spend it on me. I am undeserving.

No matter how terrible any day at school may have been, I always found such peace and love in the arms of my father and words of my mother. They loved me, and that mattered. To them, I was somebody. To them, I was smart and beautiful and funny. They didn't admire me in secret. They loved me out loud!

My mother-in-law has a prayer that she wrote for her three sons when they were children. In it, she asks God for something that I thought was incredibly bold and brilliant. In her prayer she had listed all the things she wanted for them, hopes and dreams she begged God to hear her out on. In that list of great things she longed for her sons to experience, she included one request that wasn't so typical. She asked that they would never forget what it feels like to be hurt. People who know what it feels like to ache tend to be more considerate of how they treat others. You see, pain can cause hardship, but it can also lead to growth. In a way, it is kind of like growing pains. Growth can hurt at first, but in the end, you see that it was necessary.

I can think of many Bible characters who went through these growing pains. One such example came to my mind through a parable in Luke 15:11–32. "Then He [Jesus] said: 'A certain man had two sons. And the younger of them said to his father, "Father, give me the portion of goods that falls to me" ' " (verse 11, NKJV). Already the son has committed a grave offense. It was not customary in Jewish tradition to give the inheritance until the patriarch had died. Think of it like a will. Essentially, the son says to his father, "It would be better if you were dead."

Already in my mind this changes the story. It shows a greedy, thankless, cold-hearted son disrespecting his loving, thoughtful, and gentle father.

The father had the right to expel his son from the premises empty-handed. Many parents have done so over less. At the least the father could have told him, "Who do you think you are?" and stormed off angry. He does neither. In his response, we are reminded of God's response to us—free will.

"So he divided to them his livelihood. And not many days after, the younger son gathered all together, journeyed to a far country, and there wasted his possessions with prodigal living. But when he had spent all, there arose a severe famine in that land, and he began to be in want. Then he went and joined himself to a citizen of that country, and he sent him into his fields to feed swine. And he would gladly have filled his stomach with the pods that the swine ate, and no one gave him anything" (verses 12–16, NKJV).

So here we see this rich young man who had the world at his fingertips, and then he wastes it. I can only imagine the embarrassment he must have felt when, after previously wanting for nothing, he now is applying for a job caring for pigs. It would be like the son of a CEO squandering his inheritance and then working at McDonald's. I bet that the first day he felt his stomach churning, desperate for food, his heart ached. I'm sure his memories wandered to the late-night snacks and dinner parties he had at his home with his daddy. I can just picture his eyes wandering, landing on the muck being fed to the pigs, and in the split-second that he contemplates eating it, he falls to his knees in agony.

How could he have let things get this bad? How did things spiral down so quickly? Suddenly, more than he wants money, more than he wants food, more than he wants his dignity, he wants the arms of his daddy. Because, when every other hand rejects you, there's always one palm that's wide open. When growing pains pulse through your body, peace can still be found in the embrace of the Father.

The story concludes,

But when he came to himself, he said, "How many of my father's hired servants have bread enough and to spare, and I perish with hunger! I will arise and go to my father, and will say to him, 'Father, I have sinned against heaven and before you, and I am no longer worthy to be called your son. Make me like one of your hired servants.' "

And he arose and came to his father. But when he was still a great way off, his father saw him and had compassion, and ran and fell on his neck and kissed him. And the son said to him, "Father, I have sinned against heaven and in your sight, and am no longer worthy to be called your son." But the father said to his servants, "Bring out the best robe and put it on him, and put a ring on his hand and sandals on his feet. And bring the fatted calf here and kill it, and let us eat and be merry; for this my son was dead and is alive again; he was lost and is found" (verses 17–24, NKJV).

You see, quite often it takes pain to initiate growth. Through the dark times, through the moments that we feel unworthy, we are nonetheless sons and daughters of Christ. Through toil and tears, we force ourselves to dig deep and stand. As we lie there with our face on the pavement, empty and weak, the pain too heavy to lift on our own, in that moment of fumbling and wobbling back to our feet, we grow.

The real beauty is that no matter what we've done, our heavenly Father is waiting. The second He sees us coming in His direction, He runs as fast as His legs can carry Him. He falls on our necks and kisses our dirt-stained faces. We tell Him about the pain, about our bullies, our adulteries, our mean spirit, our sexual indiscretions, our carnal addictions. We tell Him we are naked, that we are not worthy of Him. But He isn't listening. He has heard this before—ever since Eden. He's too busy placing on our backs the most beautiful robe, fastening rings to our hands, and calling for a banquet. He's sorry about the pain, but He's ecstatic about the growth. Life after Eden is realizing that life is peaks and valleys, that there is a purpose to the pressure and growth from the gravel.

When I look back on my life, I see how all the shattered dreams, tears, and secret admirers that didn't exist were a part of my growing process. They helped to mold me. All the moments I was embarrassed by my classmates made me want to give the world one less bully. I truly think I was able to polish off my own rough edges because I had felt their sting in others. I didn't want to make other people feel the way I often felt. And so I asked God to search my heart and mold me a new one. He did it for me, and He will do it for you, even in life after naked.

Pain has an incredible way of leaving imprints all over everything that it touches. Once you've felt it, you don't forget it. It causes you to reassess and figure out how you can avoid that feeling in the future. It makes you pause the next time you see someone caught in its claws because the memory of what it did to you still lingers. I'm convinced that pain is a necessary ingredient in success, and so I'm done complaining about it. I'm just ready to collapse in the arms of my Father. After all, I'm naked, and He has a robe.

Now the tax collectors and sinners were all gathering around to hear Jesus. But the Pharisees and the teachers of the law muttered, "This man welcomes sinners and eats with them."

Then Jesus told them this parable: "Suppose one of you has a hundred sheep and loses one of them. Doesn't he leave the ninety-nine in the open country and go after the lost sheep until he finds it? And when he finds it, he joyfully puts it on his shoulders and goes home. Then he calls his friends and neighbors together and says, 'Rejoice with me; I have found my lost sheep' " (verses 1–6).

*"I tell you that in the same way there will be more rejoicing in heaven over one sinner who repents than over ninety-nine righteous persons who do not need to repent"*
*(Luke 15:7).*

**Share the Naked Truth:**

1. Do you feel comfortable telling God to search your heart?

2. How has a past pain left an imprint on you?

3. In 140 characters, write an inspirational message to your followers about pain. Tweet/Facebook us *@InLifeAfterEden.*

4. Or Instagram us a photo of your favorite highlighted quote from this reading.

# Life After Naked

We are all born naked into this world, but each of
us is fully clothed in potential.
—Emmitt Smith

I vividly remember working at my school in the summer of 2004 during
the last year of my brother Tyler's life. One extremely hot day I sat on a
bright red lawnmower, racing back and forth, weaving in and out of old
rusty playground equipment. I was so completely engrossed in the lyrics
playing on my music player that I didn't notice Tyler coming. I nearly
ran him over as he powered across the lawn in his electric wheelchair and
slowly approached me. Idling down the mower, I removed my ear buds.
I'll never forget that look on his face as he mumbled under his breath, "I
thought you might be thirsty."

Gulping down the lemonade, I returned the glass to him. He placed it
in the wire basket strapped to the front of his wheelchair, smoothly slid his
grip firmly around the handles for stability, and he strolled off back to our
campus house a few hundred yards away.

In that moment, everything clicked. Tyler presented me with his gift
of gratitude in the form of a glass of lemonade. He was telling me "thank
you" for all the times I got up extra early to bathe him before heading
off to school. It was his way of thanking me for driving him to all of his
appointments, therapies, and doctor visits. For being a shoulder to cry on
when he was feeling discouraged. He taught me something beautiful that
day—a simple glass of lemonade was all that he could give to return the

countless moments I had helped him in his struggle with cancer. As his image began to disappear in the distance, becoming consumed by the sun casting its glare upon the pavement, I sat there in the silence of the summer heat, listening to the hum of the electric motor fade with distance.

He was dying. His skin was pale, and his face was swollen from the chemo treatments. His legs were lifeless and frail as they lay against the stiff bars that screamed of their uselessness. Watching him leave me there in the middle of that old playground, I knew it was just a matter of time before he would confront his final battle of faith. Tears began to stream down my dusty cheeks, leaving a visible trail as they fell into my lap, vanishing within the stitching of my tattered jeans. To my right sat that rusty swing set with its corroded chains and ripped seats. What I would have given that day to sit side by side with my brother in that old swing set, meaninglessly pumping our legs back and forth together in a perfect motion. Laughing, we would bask in the rays from above without a single worry in this life after Eden.

As much his loss haunts me, and as much as the suffering in your life haunts you, if we keep our eyes on Christ we can endure anything. After all, this life is but a moment.

Dr. Coldwell shared these alarming statistics when it comes to the field of cancer. In one of his prominent interviews he said, "We have the cancer rate of 7% in 1900, and we have a cancer rate of 51% today. Every second person in America has cancer, or will get cancer. In a family of 4 statistically 2 of them will get cancer." The statistics are in. The facts are published. Everyone living in today's world either has cancer, will get cancer, or knows someone in their close circle with cancer.

This horrible disease has defined all too many with the acronym RIP. Cancer is a plague that not only affects the physical body but plays on the psyche. People who have had cancer in the past will wonder on a daily basis if it's going to come back. Little boys and girls whose biggest obstacle should be figuring out how to ride with no training wheels instead grapple with a different kind of courage altogether—the courage to endure radiation, MRIs, and doctor visits. While the rest of the world is busy adjusting the covers on their iPhones, cancer patients are deciding which bandana will best conceal their nakedness.

It's everyone's worst fear. Just when you thought you were "in the clear," you're bombarded with an X-ray that reveals the truth. Cancer operates at the highest level of intelligence. It's a trained assassin that strikes under the cover of darkness with calculated precision. If 51 percent of the people living in the United States will get cancer in their lifetime, there is only one thing left to do: flip a coin, and hope that cancer doesn't win the toss.

My brother was an incredible young man who was forced to play in this game of heads and tails. It's a game of odds, and cancer dictates the rules. "Heads I win, tails you lose." For Tyler, the chore of putting on a pair of pants was overwhelming at times. Cancer numbed his ability to feel from the waist down, forcing him to trade in his car keys for a wheelchair.

His life went from daydream to nightmare in a single moment. As the doctor placed the film on the projector, no words were needed. The obvious mass pressing against his spine was unmistakable. For Tyler the famous expression "A picture is worth a thousand words" held an undesired new meaning that day. The jury was in, and the gavel's thud echoed a vibration that would leave us speechless. Cancer was the victor. He put up a good fight, though. No one could argue that much. Not even cancer.

He was sentenced to solitary confinement. His cell bed was a synthetic pad held together by meticulously woven threading. The lifeless steel of his hospice bars fastened to the side rails of his bed hugged his even more unresponsive legs. How does one deal with such news? First he had to deal with the loss of feeling in his lower extremities, and then cancer screamed in his ear, "Soon you will lose feeling altogether!" If this was you, with just a few months left to live, what choices would you make?

In the summer of 2004, cancer handed him his death sentence in the form of a black-and-white image neatly tucked inside a manila envelope, as if this were something he wanted to place in the important document section of his filing cabinet. If all was stripped away from you in a split second, how would this alter your view of this life? Your view of God? Your view of your purpose in this world?

Growing up, Tyler was just like any other kid who loved to run and scream at the top of his lungs. During his early teenage years, people became enamored by Tyler's impartiality when it came to choosing his friends. It didn't matter what you looked like; if you crossed paths with him, he wouldn't let you slip by without saying "hello." When you meet someone like Tyler, you don't forget it. People of his caliber give off a unique vibe that can't be faked or fabricated. It's authentic. His genuine approach to life was one of his biggest character strengths as he matured.

He was also quite the ladies' man. It was rumored that he always seemed to have a pack of gorgeous girls surrounding him—until cancer entered the picture. With life being as tough as it is, some people seem to have it even tougher. No longer able to run the town at odd hours of the night with his friends, Tyler felt lost. Eventually he got a phone call from the Make a Wish Foundation. He took that big check and wheeled himself right through the doors of Best Buy. He decided that he was going to pass his time engrossed in the latest technology.

He got every movie, videogame, and high-tech gadget you could imagine. Who could blame him? He was going to spend day after day alone in his bedroom while the rest of the world was occupied with "bad hair days" and "nothing to wear." He knew that his life was only going to get worse as the cancer spread. He knew he would eventually get to the point where he couldn't even get out of bed because the pain would be too great.

As the clock ticked, Tyler soon realized that theater-sized flat-screen televisions weren't big enough to fill the even bigger void inside his heart. This is when a slow shift took place in Tyler's life. With the curtains soon to close, he decided that he wanted to confide in something else or in someone else—God. He didn't want RIP to be last thing people remembered of him. He wanted to leave a legacy that would never fade with time.

Tyler started engaging in Bible study and became convicted that he needed to get baptized before he died. Bloated from chemotherapy, and paralyzed from the waist down, he was carried into the baptismal tank. With tears rolling down his cheeks, Tyler rejoiced. Not because his pain was gone, or because his condition was on the upside. He rejoiced because he knew that someday he was going to rejoin the ones he loved.

Something happens when our backs are against the wall. We do one of two things: fight or flight. Tyler decided that day, at his baptism, that he was going to fight. He decided this was his moment, and he was going to have the last laugh. Sure, cancer was going to win the battle, but Tyler had purposed that he was going to win the war. The devil could take his body, but he would allow God to claim his soul.

In the last moments of his life here on this diseased and dying planet we call home, something supernatural happened. To this day it sends shivers up my spine, because it was the day that I could no longer deny that God, Satan, and this war over our lives is real. Hours before my brother died, Tyler did three amazing things. He came out of his two-day coma and said these words: "Hurry, give me the phone!" Then he dialed every one of his family and close friends and pleaded with them. He only stayed on the phone for a few minutes each time he made a new call, but he wanted everyone to hear these words: "At all costs, you have to be in heaven." Finally, he turned to each of us in the room, he pulled every person individually to his side.

Whispering in my ear on his deathbed, Tyler mustered up the strength one last time to give his last words. He told me, "Brother, at all costs you've got to be there." Slipping back into the coma, he lay motionless. We were all sure this was it. In tears we huddled close, hoping this was some horrible dream that we would all awake from.

However, one more phenomenon occurred. Out of the coma-like state that he seemed to have drifted back into, Tyler suddenly began to shake his head back and forth as if two voices were at odds inside his head. Then, without warning, in a loud voice, he cried out these words, "JESUS IS MY KING! SATAN GET YOUR UGLY FACE OUT OF THIS ROOM!" And then he shook his head back and forth one more time and repeated what he had just said. "JESUS IS MY KING! SATAN GET YOUR UGLY FACE OUT OF THIS ROOM!" Then my brother stopped breathing.

We were devastated and God-smacked at the same time. Tyler had taught us so much about what it means to be a true Christian. True Christians will find themselves immersed in the grip of suffering and still proclaim that God is good.

My brother died two days after his eighteenth birthday on November 18, 2004. Even though it has been just over a decade since he breathed his last earthly breath, I have never forgotten his words, "At all costs you've got to be there." The statistics are in, and the facts are published. Everyone living in today's world either has cancer, will get cancer, or knows someone in their close circle with cancer. For many of us, the obstacles may win the battle, but Christians win the war.

Dear reader, at all costs, you and I have to be there! My brother showed me that this life is truly but a moment. Our nakedness is but a moment, our suffering, our pain, our shame is all but a moment . . . and we can endure anything for a moment. Can't we?

Let Jesus be your King.

> " 'And God will wipe away every tear from their eyes; there shall be no more death, nor sorrow, nor crying. There shall be no more pain, for the former things have passed away.' Then He who sat on the throne said, 'Behold, I make all things new.' And He said to me, 'Write, for these words are true and faithful' " (Revelation 21:4, 5, NKJV).

**Share the Naked Truth:**

1. What is the legacy you want to leave?

2. If you were told you had a few months to live, would you change the way you are living?

3. In 140 characters, write a message for your tombstone. On Tyler's it says, "The best is yet to come." Tweet/Facebook us *@InLifeAfterEden*.

4. Or Instagram us a photo of your favorite highlighted quote from this reading.

# Dear Cancer: You Are Dying

To die, to sleep.
To sleep, perchance to dream—ay, there's the rub,
For in that sleep of death what dreams may come.
—William Shakespeare

Rainy days often remind me of the darkness and sadness that exist within our world. I am a grown adult woman, and yet on rainy days I feel like I am an eight-year-old girl who wishes Grandpa could take her fishing. Recently, I went to visit my grandfather's grave with my children, mother, and grandmother. My grandmother's eyes had brightened when I asked if we could visit the grave—I think it feels good when she is reminded that she is not the only one missing him. As we stood at the headstone, my daughter asked me to help her "open it." She was two years old. She thought that if we could just lift the headstone off the ground, then Grandpa would appear. My grandmother's eyes watered.

A friend of mine lost her husband in a motorcycle accident while I was studying during a three-week intensive in Europe. I was visiting new sites and posting photos to my social media accounts, and she was curled up on the floor wondering how her world could stop and yet keep spinning.

Sometimes when I stop to think about all my grandfather has missed, I wonder that too. After my grandpa's funeral, my family ate in the church commons area, where they had set up lunch. I wasn't hungry. I was pregnant with my son at the time, and I remember going to my grandmother's house later and sitting in my grandpa's favorite chair and just thinking how cruel it was that someone who had been such a pivotal person my life would never even meet my son. It made me sick.

I was told in elementary school that Christopher Columbus died in 1506. In Spain stands a monument to the great discoverer. In my opinion, the most interesting piece of this tribute is a statue of a lion destroying one of the Latin words that had been part of Spain's motto for centuries. You see, before "1492 when Columbus sailed the ocean blue," the Spaniards thought they had reached the outer limits of the earth. They believed the world was flat and that if you traversed too far, you would fall off the edge. They believed they had reached that edge, and so their motto was *Ne Plus Ultra*, which means "(go) no more beyond."

On the sign at Columbus's memorial they've put the statue of the lion destroying the Latin word *Ne*, or "no." And now the sign reads *Plus Ultra*. Columbus proved that there was indeed "more beyond."

Paul tells us, "We shall all be changed—in a moment, in the twinkling of an eye, at the last trumpet. For the trumpet will sound, and the dead will be raised incorruptible, and we shall be changed" (1 Corinthians 15:51, 52, NKJV).

You see, Paul, like Columbus, knew that there was more beyond. I have been filled with a certain kind of permanent sadness since losing my grandpa. Every time I see my grandmother, I take note of what we have lost. And yet, my heart swells when I focus on the promise of God—a promise that Grandpa knew well. It is the promise of 1 Corinthians 15:51, 52. It is the promise that when our Savior returns, Grandpa's grave will burst open and he will leap out. A trumpet will sound, and he will rise incorruptible, and changed.

I love walking through the cemetery. We have one a mile or so from our house, and I walk with my husband there often. I like to imagine what that yard will look like when Jesus returns. A place filled with tears and sadness will become one of the biggest beacons of joy. Isn't that just like God? Bringing life where death rests, and converting sadness into joy.

There is more beyond. And so while we can feel sadness about the time we don't have with our loved ones while we are still here on this earth, we can also smile and think of all the new memories that await us in our Father's kingdom. *Plus Ultra* is the mantra that gets me through rainy days. I am ready for Jesus to return for me, because I believe that there is more beyond.

Sometimes I dream of what life will look like when Jesus vanquishes sin, when we are no longer naked. The moment I cannot wait for is the one when Jesus tells disease and sadness, death and pain that they are dying. I cannot wait for God to grab cancer by the horns and banish it forever. And so, I penned a letter to cancer, because I believe that there is more beyond:

Dear Cancer,

My husband and I were on a walk the other afternoon. Out of no-where I saw tears form in his eyes. I didn't have to ask what he was thinking about. I could tell by his vacant stare that it was you. You changed his life in the fall of 2004. His brother introduced the two of you. He was only eighteen years old. Do you remember Tyler? He was handsome, athletic, and popular. He always knew just what to say and had this uncanny ability to make everyone around him feel as though they were the most important person in his world. You snuffed a light out of my husband and his family the day that you took Tyler. You didn't just take Tyler. You took them too.

I think it may be kind of like a person who suffers a traumatic ac-cident and loses a limb. People keep telling you that you are *lucky* to be alive, but of all the words in the dictionary, you'd be hard-pressed to find an adjective less fitting. They told my husband that time heals all wounds, and this is the lie that has made him feel like a freak for over a decade. Surely something must be wrong with him. Why can't he just get over it? Because unless you are the one that dies, you don't get over death; you live it. I think what happens is, the more time that goes by, the more people stop asking how you are doing. And let's face it, no one wants to hear the real answer anyway. No one wants to hear that sometimes when you sleep you awake to the sounds of your own screams. No one really wants to know that the degree of separa-tion between nine years and right now is nine seconds. He doesn't live life by hours or days; he lives life by seconds, by sounds, by pictures, by a familiar face in the distance that never materializes. But they told him he'd get over it. I'm not convinced that time heals much of anything. I think people just stop asking. Either that or he stopped being honest.

My grandmother met you in the month of February. You are such a cruel antagonist to pick on such a sweet old lady. My grandfather introduced you. He is gone now, but she's not, and yet in many ways she is. You took away the man she laid beside for sixty years. For sixty years she made eggs sunny-side up because that was how he liked them. For seven months those cracked eggs have been her only sunny days. I try to call her often.

"How are you?" I ask her.

"Lonely," she responds.

My uncle, my mother, her grandchildren all love her, and call her, and visit her, and yet she can't help but feel lonely. In a room full of family she is still lonely, and on her face I see yours. She hates you. I think you should know that my grandpa was special. A month before he died, I gave him a copy of one of my books that I had dedicated to him. I loved him intensely, and I wanted him to know it. He took that book and placed it in the beltline of his pants. For weeks, every gas station attendant, sales clerk, or waiter was forced to feel the binding of that book pressed into their hands.

"My granddaughter wrote this book," he'd say. "She's a writer." They'd smile out of compliance, but he wasn't finished. "Read the dedication," he'd urge them sternly, and as the world hustled around them, his froze one more time. They'd read the words I penned, and when they finished, he was satisfied. They'd push the book back to him, and he'd place it into his pants again. I can still feel the warmth of my smile watching him approach strangers over and over while wrestling that book into their hands. If I'd known that you were lying silently inside of him like a warrior in a bush, I would have written him a thousand more dedications. That book sits on his nightstand now. No one has touched it. Not even me. My grandma would, but I am pretty sure she worries that if she felt it, instead of the smooth cover, all her fingers would grab is loneliness.

## Dear Cancer: You Are Dying

I loved him. Did you know that, cancer? Did you know that I even loved the smell of the wood of his toothpick? I miss that smell. And I miss seeing that book tucked into his pants. You robbed me of a man of mythical proportions. And this Thanksgiving, at a table full of people, beneath the laughter and the love, my grandmother will still be lonely.

I have friends who have met you too, introduced to you by their fathers, mothers, sisters, and friends. You raped them. You robbed them of their virginity and left the cruel taste of emptiness. You're like a stain on their once bright white shirts. They try all the different methods to scrub you out of their lives. Some haven't even tried to erase you, while others have scraped at you till their knuckles bleed. But if I am being honest, on certain days, in certain light, I can still see them wearing you. Do you know what it feels like to lace yourself every day with something you hate? A friend of mine has freshly put you on, and no matter how many layers she is smothered with, all she ever feels is cold. She misses her daddy. Because for little girls, no matter what they wear or how they look, daddies always make them feel pretty. She's beautiful. And I wonder if she still knows it. She hates you.

There's a fifteen-year-old girl in a town nearby who is currently fighting you. My friend called and asked me to pray for a girl I didn't know. When she said that it was you who had showed up again, unwanted and unannounced, I prayed immediately. I prayed that she'd beat you. I'd love to see you get the snot kicked out of you by a fifteen-year-old girl. I hope everyone who reads this prays that in the midst of this struggle, Sarah will rise and stand over you. She'll place her heel in the heart of your chest and join the survivors who echo, "Dear cancer, you lose!"

And then in ignorance or stupidity someone has the audacity to tell them that "this is God's plan." The advice of fools shouldn't smell so strong. You were never a part of God's plan! Disease, sickness, death, abandonment, pain, and despair were not stains that He fashioned. How dare they insinuate that *He* made *you*? Only out of ignorance do they hang those chains on God. The weight is so heavy He could

snap beneath them. But they need someone to blame, and so in vain
He wears them.

Was it not He that suffered in order to end suffering? Was it not
His hands that were pierced so that He could hold ours? They pulled
out the hair of His beard and pressed hard into his scalp a crown of
thorns that He wore with pride, because in doing so, He defeated
you. He hates you just as much as we do! Your stench is so foul that
He had to isolate this world from the rest of the heavens. Through
mercy He advocates for us. Through compassion He holds us together while we recite over and over again for anyone who will listen
about the day that you killed us while we remained breathing. You
killed us. Yet somehow you left us breathing. He beat you, and yet
over and over people attach your name to His. How dare they! You
were never a part of His plan. Somewhere Satan is laughing.

Dear cancer, you should know there is one thought that relieves
me. You're dying. My Lord has sentenced you. As I thought of all the
lives that you've destroyed, I thought it was imperative to remind you,
and everyone else, that your days, cancer, are numbered. My King is
coming back, and while many of us have been so wrecked by you that
we cannot see through darkness, I hope this may shed the smallest
light. Because Jesus, the One they called Christ, has conquered you.

Matthew 25:6 says, "And at midnight, a cry was heard: 'Behold,
the bridegroom cometh!' " (NKJV). I long for the still of night when
I am awakened by such a shout, when the nightmares that plague
my husband will be burned by the blaze of His chariot. Cancer, you
are dying! Paul tells us in 1 Corinthians 15:51, 52, "We shall all be
changed—in a moment, in the twinkling of an eye, at the last trumpet. For the trumpet will sound, and the dead will be raised incorruptible, and we shall be changed" (NKJV).

You cancer, you are dying, but we shall all be made new! The heavens will rumble, voices that you silenced will cry out in victory, and
children that you tortured will burst from their graves! People won't
even know the meaning of the word *lonely*. Lives that you claimed
will be reclaimed by my Jesus, and on that day, cancer, you will die.
And that is why Paul writes in verse 54, "Death is swallowed up in

victory." The grave of Christ swallowed you, cancer, and in a brazen tone Paul mocks you when he finishes in verse 55, "O Death, where is your sting? O Hades, where is your victory?"

All this time while we wept, we forgot how the story actually ends, because, while we die once, we will live again forever! The faces of those whom we love, the saints who lived naked before us, will shine brighter than the morning, and just as darkness runs at the sight of light, so shall you scramble in the face of our Jesus. We will live again, but cancer, you will die forever. You will die alone, you will die cold, and no one will be at your funeral. Cancer, you will be the one who finds out the meaning of the word *lonely*.

Dear cancer, because of Jesus, you are dying.

*"Where, O death, is your victory? Where,*
*O death, is your sting?" (1 Corinthians 15:55).*

## Share the Naked Truth:

1. Has cancer impacted the life of you or someone you love?

2. Why does God allow diseases such as cancer to infiltrate His saints?

3. In 140 characters, write a message to a cancer survivor or someone in its grip. Tweet/Facebook us *@InLifeAfterEden.*

4. Or Instagram us a photo of your favorite highlighted quote from this reading.

# Epilogue: Stepping Back in Eden

When everything is ready, I will come and get you, so that
you will always be with me where I am (John 14:3, NLT).

Parking your car, you take another look in the rearview mirror before
exiting your vehicle. When your feet hit the pavement, a deep swallow of
breath warms your chest. The breeze tumbles through your hair, and the
sun kisses your skin.

"It's a beautiful night," you think to yourself while walking to the door
with a dance in your step. Once inside, you stroll across the room. The
peace is overwhelming, and the joy is nearly indescribable. There are a lot
of people here, and the music is blaring. You use your arms when you talk
and tell jokes that leave the room in a roar. All eyes are on you, and it feels
good to be noticed. It feels right to be seen. You were made for this. All
of us were.

Then, the Father walks in. The angels' wings grow still, and someone
puts the music on silent. Your chest heaves at being this close to such
warmth and beauty. Your heart pounds because of the joy that pulses
through it like the thud of a drum. The Savior looks right at you. He steps
back and grins, and it feels so good to have His eyes on you.

"How do you like the robe?" He asks with a nod of satisfaction.

"Fits like a glove," you respond, proud and poised, before lowering your
head to acknowledge His work.

As you look around the room, you notice the most beautiful light. The
robes are spotless, and the crispness of their white is so bright, you know

you would squint if you were in any other form.

Your friends are here. All of them. The uncles you looked up to, the parents you missed, and the baby you lost, who squeals with delight after being placed back in your arms. There is a bouquet of fresh roses sitting perfectly on a long table, and you notice something breathtaking—no thorns.

Adam and Eve make their way through the room, embracing each person and fawning over the little ones. There is no sign of pain here. No symbol of death, and no icons of shame. Everything is beautiful, everything is perfect, no hairs are out of place, and Eden is restored. Then wings flap, and violins play, and you hear the softest melody. Slowly but proudly, Jesus raises His hands. And then you realize: there is still one symbol of death, one sign of pain, one icon of shame: His hands.

The scars tell the story of a life before this one. A world where hope was nearly crushed and dreams slowly suffocated. Tears well in your eyes as you smell the hair of that beautiful baby you prayed that you would one day be able to hold again . . . and here you are.

This is heaven; and the only rose still bearing thorns is the palms of Jesus Christ. A forever reminder of the sacrifice made so that we all could be here; clothed in the glory of God. We share war stories that you'd swear were fables had you not known intimately what it felt like to breathe, walk, live, and die in a world very far from this one. It's all a distant memory now; the tips of your fingers give off heat, and the smile on your face is genuine . . .

Friends, a time will come when it's almost hard to remember what it was like in this life after Eden.

> *"People will come from east and west and north and south,*
> *and will take their places at the feast in the kingdom of God.*
> *Indeed there are those who are last who will be first,*
> *and first who will be last" (Luke 13:29, 30).*

## Share the Naked Truth:

1. What does life after Eden mean to you?

2. Is there any way we can "clothe" ourselves while we await full restoration?

3. In 140 characters, write what life after Eden looks like in your own life. Tweet/Facebook us *@InLifeAfterEden*.

4. Or Instagram us a photo of your favorite highlighted quote from this reading.